Texas Eccentrics

John Kuhn

ISBN
1-933177-12-8 (10 digit)
978-1-933177-12-0 (13 digit)

Library of Congress Control Number 2008938329

First Edition

Printed in the United States of America

Published by Atriad Press LLC
13820 Methuen Green
Dallas, TX 75240
(972) 671-0002
www.atriadpress.com

Dedication

To my absolutely perfect wife, Noelia, who doesn't realize how wonderful she is because her husband doesn't know how to tell her.

And to my kids—Noah, Evan, and Liliana—for the many smiles they throw my way on a typical day, a fact which, now that I think about it, makes a typical day pretty dang special.

Thanks also to Sherry Brown for telling me I should write, and to Dennis Menese, for drawing the great illustrations found in this book.

Table of Contents

Foreword

In Hunter Publishing's *Adventure Guide to Texas*, author Kimberly Young credits the Lone Star State with creating "an aura around the world of unabashed quirkiness…" She then goes on to tell the story of the eccentric Amarillo millionaire who paid a group of artists to bury a bunch of Cadillacs, rear bumpers to the sky, in a line beside Interstate 40. Call it a crazy man's Stonehenge, if you will.

If Texas were like any other state, that story would be the weirdest one in this book.

It's not.

Texas Eccentrics shares the sometimes amusing, sometimes heart-rending stories of real-life Texas eccentrics, from two-time presidential candidate H. Ross Perot to abominable snowman hunter Tom Slick to the man behind Amarillo's "Cadillac Ranch," Stanley Marsh 3. Also included are one-time world's richest man Howard Hughes, Charlie Wilson (Tom Hanks' character in the award-winning film *Charlie Wilson's War*), Kinky Friedman (the Texas candidate who put the "goober" in "gubernatorial"), round-ball goofball Dennis Rodman, and dozens of others. The fact that there were so many to choose from when compiling this book is testament to the pervasiveness of eccentricity in Texas society.

The Texas eccentric is such a well-known and fascinating character in our culture, in fact, that it has become an archetype in both American literature and film. Bizarre Texans have been featured in the hilarious play *Greater Tuna*, in 1980s television series *J.J. Starbuck* and *Alice* (remember Flo?), and in Hollywood films such as *The Astronaut Farmer, Holes,* and *Secondhand Lions*. The popular concept of the Texas eccentric, it appears, is firmly rooted in real-life. And the fictionalized weird Texans are no stranger than many real-life weird Texans, not to mention weird adopted Texans, of which

1

Foreword

there are more than a few.

The nutty Texan has given rise not only to some memorable fictional roles, but also to some good jokes. In one of them, an "eccentric Texas millionaire" hosts a party and shows off an alligator he's placed in his swimming pool. He offers one million dollars to anyone who will swim from one end of the pool to another. Just then, there's a splash. Everyone looks and sees the local Baptist preacher swimming across the pool, the gator snapping at his heels. He climbs out of the pool just in time and everyone cheers. The millionaire asks him if he wants his money in big bills or small bills. The preacher says, "I just want the name of whichever blankity-blank pushed me into the pool."

The eccentric Texan, real or imagined, plays an important role in Lone Star society. Outsiders sometimes imagine the Lone Star populace as a homogeneous band of conservative cowboy ruffians—especially since the Presidency of former Texas governor George W. Bush—but the reality of modern-day Texas is quite different. It isn't just the stick-in-the-mud neighbor of Georgia O'Keefe's avant-garde New Mexico, a state replete with alternative energy sources, alternative medicines, and alternative lifestyles, with UFOlogists, art galleries, and a pending spaceport.

No, there's more to Texas. While yes, it's home to about a zillion Baptist deacons, it's also home to its fair share of artists, singer-songwriters, cross-dressers, Beatles fans, Libertarians, Prius drivers, and other odd ducks. In fact, the most culturally sensitive New Yorker would probably be shocked if he were to spend just one weekend on Austin's Sixth Street intermingling with the spur-clad cowboys and the stiletto-clad transvestites who prowl those legendary sidewalks—shocked, in all likelihood, at the sheer inaccuracy of his preconceived notions about the Lone Star State.

The mayor of Austin has referred to something he calls the "confluence of hippie and redneck culture." This melding of

2

two extremes makes the Lone Star State unlike any other. Some people talk about red states, blue states, and those all-important purple states. Texas, though, is a bright red state with equally bright blue polka dots. Nonconformists here don't have the luxury of surrounding themselves with other nonconformists. Texas' tolerant folks don't just tolerate the certifiably weird; they also have to tolerate boot-wearing bankers, mega-church members, bow hunters, and fans of talk radio.

The Texas eccentric is the living, breathing embodiment of the ideal that Texas must not and cannot be defined in simplistic terms. Nuance, it turns out, can be readily found in a place where people say things like "y'all" and "fixin' to."

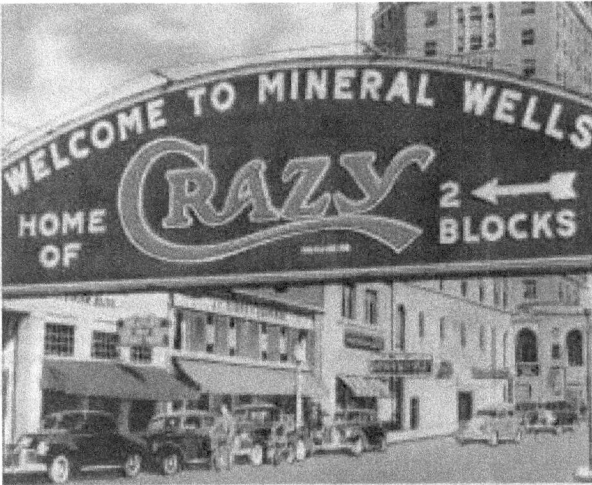

It is perhaps mere coincidence that the author of this book lives in a town that for many years displayed a huge sign over its main thoroughfare which read, "Welcome to Mineral Wells, Home of Crazy." True, the "Crazy" on the sign referred specifically to a brand of cure-all mineral water that made Mineral Wells into a 1920's boomtown (and is still sold here by the Famous Water Company, by the way). But the sign was surely intended as a *double entendre*. Sure, Mineral Wells was home to the Crazy brand water crystals that cured everything from rheumatism to delirium, but what made the sign funny was what it implied, that the town was home to another kind of crazy, the kind of crazy you can't bottle. The kind that is apparently pretty widely distributed throughout Texas.

Texas is a state with a river—the Nueces—whose name in Spanish means "nuts." We in Texas have convinced ourselves it was named after the pecan trees growing wild along its banks. I suspect otherwise. Texas is a state that is the proud home of the world's fourth-largest Eiffel tower and second-largest pecan. It's a state whose early denizens chose town names like Cut and Shoot, Noodle, Gun Barrel City, Happy, Loco, Nameless, Tarzan, and Bug Tussle. One shouldn't be the least bit surprised to find a collection of wacky characters in its annals.

Eccentricity reached Texas long before electricity, after all. And like electricity, it has since found its way to every corner of the state. In fact, a Texan who can't name an eccentric member of the family probably *is* the eccentric member of the family. And almost every Texas town boasts its very own odd character, some strange somebody who serves as a sort of informal town mascot—the guy who rides a lawnmower all over town, for example, or the lady on the three-wheeled bike with the basket on the front brimming with aluminum cans.

But eccentricity isn't all bad. Many of the folks profiled in these pages have found great success in business, politics, sports, and other areas. Some became world-famous, in spite of (or perhaps because of) their wackiness. Between them, they have done much to make Texas what it is. Eccentricity, in the end, isn't just another word for weirdness. It's also the cousin of daring, of bravado, of going-against-the-flow. Eccentricity is no more kin to insanity than it is to audacity.

The future of Texas—and of Texas eccentricity—is bright. A big seller in the state capital since 2000 has been t-shirts and

4

bumper stickers emblazoned with the unofficial motto of the city: "Keep Austin Weird." And, apparently, the "Keep Austin Weird" movement is working—in a 2004 interview with the *Daily Texan,* Austin mayor Will Wynn reported that Austinites regularly show up at city council meetings in costumes and present grievances and concerns in the form of songs, poems, and "interpretive dance."

While Austin is indeed an eclectic place, it doesn't have a monopoly on Texas eccentricity. Wesley Treat, in his introduction to the book *Weird Texas,* referred to Texans in general when he wrote "there's...something we've got a whole lot of—weirdness."

And so we do. Here's hoping you enjoy reading about some of Texas' most colorful characters in these pages.

Writing from the "Home of Crazy,"

John Kuhn

Foreword

Part 1
Bizarre Businesspeople

Over the years, Texas has been a major center for booms in the cattle industry, the banking industry, the oil industry, the aerospace industry, and the hi-tech industry. Texans have launched some of the most financially successful businesses in history in the above mentioned fields and others, and the people at the helm of these businesses have—on occasion—been a little quirky.

The individuals profiled in *Part 1 – Bizarre Businesspeople* include two men who at different times each became the world's richest man. Most are or were millionaires or billionaires. They include oilmen, cattle and land barons, a computer programmer or two, and a few real estate investors. Some inherited wealth; others built their own from nothing. And others didn't quite strike it rich at all. Some were born in Texas. Others "got here as quickly as they could," as the old saying goes. And, though they've found a home in this section, some of them could have fit just as easily in another part of this book, having been, in addition to businesspeople, dabblers in politics or the arts.

There is only one thing every last one of them has in common: in one way or another, they are all just a little bit different than the average person.

Okay, a couple of them are more than just "a little bit" different.

The "eccentric Texas millionaire" has made regular appearances in books, movies, and on television. The rich crazy uncle is a handy plot device, I suppose, and writers apparently have a hard time resisting the temptation of giving this character boots and a cowboy hat.

But in this section we'll see that truth is indeed often

stranger than fiction. We will learn about the real people who have inspired a cliché by virtue of the incredible lives they've led. In the end, we may well find that the same quality that drove early settlers to risk it all by coming to untamed Texas has lived on. It has found refuge in the hearts of a few intrepid pioneers of enterprise. By some, this quality may be called foolhardiness; by others bravery; by still others audacity. But we're happy to call it by its real name: Texas eccentricity.

Chapter 1

"Biosphere Benefactor"

Ed Bass
c. 1945-present

Name: Edward Perry Bass
Lived: c. 1945-present
Texas connection: Lives in Fort Worth
Occupation: Real estate developer and environmental do-gooder
Claim to weirdness: Spent $200 million on a giant glass bubble in the Arizona desert
Tex-centricity Scale: 4 giant snow globes (out of 10)

Edward P. Bass, son of Perry Bass and grandnephew of pioneering Texas wildcatter Sid Richardson, inherited a fortune along with his three brothers. He is a member of one of the most prominent oil and gas dynasties in Texas. According to *Forbes* magazine, Bass was the 645th richest man in the world in 2006, with an estimated worth of $1.2 billion.

The Bass family is most famous, recently, for having given the people of Ft. Worth the beautiful Nancy Lee and Perry R. Bass Performance Hall, a downtown symphony hall complete with giant angels blowing golden horns adorning its exterior walls. Since its opening in 1988, this dazzling structure has attracted world-class performers to Ft. Worth. However, son Edward has been involved in a number of other enterprises besides Bass Hall, from real estate investing to philanthropy. And then there's that one little project in Arizona....

Never having had to work, Ed Bass has devoted much of his life to ecology and environmental causes. The more orthodox of his ecological activities include serving as chairman of the executive committee of the World Wildlife Fund and on the boards of the New York Botanical Garden, the Botanical Research Institute of Texas, the African Wildlife Foundation, and the Jane Goodall Institute for Wildlife Research, Education, and Conservation.

Then there are the less orthodox ventures, like Biosphere 2.

As a graduate-level architecture student at Yale University, Edward Bass built adobe houses in New Mexico. While there, he met a man named John Allen, the eclectic founder of Synergia Ranch. According to one biographer, Allen "preached the virtues of ... 'spaceship earth.'"

Fast forward to 1991, the year Bass' most ambitious ecological venture became a concrete (and steel and glass) reality. The management team of Biosphere 2 sealed eight willing participants inside an eight-story structure in the Arizona desert and left them to survive on their own. If the experiment went as planned, there would be no outside interference whatsoever.

News outlets covered Biosphere 2 to the point of total media saturation. This was something different. Something daring. The inhabitants were to stay for two years with no outside influence. Biosphere 2 was supposed to generate all the

10

food, water, and air the inhabitants would need for their entire stay.

The project had a variety of implications. Leaders hoped it would further the study of earth's interrelated ecosystems and also provide important information about the mechanics of future space colonization. It was hoped that Biosphere 2 would answer a very important question in the affirmative—can mankind create a self-sustaining closed system capable of supporting human life indefinitely?

When asked why he invested somewhere between $150 million and $200 million of his fortune in Biosphere 2, Ed Bass said he believed the project "had tremendous potential to develop technologies, know-how, data" and that it would "have great use in environmental matters on all scales, from the fairly small to the planetary. And in a business sense, I saw that these technologies would have a very significant commercial application."

That, my friends, is called optimism.

In retrospect, the project can only fairly be described as a colossal failure. The food produced inside the habitat quickly proved inadequate for the inhabitants—they basically survived on bananas, the only really successful food plant inside the structure—and they eventually had to break into an emergency food supply in order to survive. Worse still, two infusions of pure oxygen were required inside the habitat, as the plant life inside did not produce enough O_2 to counteract the carbon dioxide produced by microbes in the soil.

As things headed south inside Biosphere 2, personal conflicts erupted between the inhabitants; they formed factions within the dome. Biosphere 2 became little more than a giant snow globe full of bananas and hatred. The team members had differences of opinion about several things, principal among them the purpose of the project. Those who felt that the purpose of Biosphere 2 was to conduct research wanted to scuttle the self-sufficiency approach and accept food and oxygen from the outside. They wanted to continue their research unimpeded for the entire two years. But others felt that the whole point of the experiment was for the inhabitants to survive for two years with no outside influence, and they didn't want any intervention whatsoever. Accepting outside help meant mission failure to them.

The interpersonal conflicts were so bad that many of the inhabitants stopped speaking to one another and parted ways as soon as they were let out of the structure. Scientists can be prickly that way.

The outcome of Biosphere 2 is eerily reminiscent of television experiments in which subjects are placed in a closed environment and subjected to a variety of stressors. *Big Brother*, in particular, comes to mind, as do a whole host of others, including *Survivor, The Ultimate Fighter,* and *The Surreal Life*. It doesn't take a real leap to imagine a young John de Mol watching the news in 1993, seeing the Biosphere inhabitants emerge, and having a light bulb come on. *Big Brother* started initial development in the Netherlands in 1997. Could it be? Is it possible that Ed Bass inadvertently invented reality TV? If so, the Biosphere was more influential than many thought. And Bass should be punished.

A second attempt at habitation inside Biosphere 2 fared even worse than the first one. Less than a month into the second project, armed agents removed the management team from the premises of Biosphere 2—it was *Nova* meets *Cops*. With the mad scientists out of the way, Ed Bass' company took over the day-to-day operation of the experiment. Four days later, two members of the original crew returned to Biosphere 2; they opened all the doors and the experiment was ruined. The project continued, but in the ensuing months two members of the team inside quit the project and, after six months, the project was cancelled.

Criticism of the project was plentiful—outsiders speculated that Biosphere management "cheated" by introducing outside food and air without reporting it, though proof of such cheating never appeared. Others claimed that the whole thing was little more than a media stunt. Nevertheless, despite the negative reactions to the exercise, the Biosphere 2 project did indeed make important contributions to science. The study of "confined space psychology" was advanced by what happened inside the giant glass dome, and scientists looking ahead to space exploration were reminded that building a self-sustaining space base would not be as easy as science fiction authors might make it seem.

The scientific value of Mr. Bass' vast investment is further emphasized by the fact that two different universities have lent their expertise to the project in recent years. Columbia University took over management of the site after the second mission ended prematurely in 1995, and the University of Arizona took over management in 2007. They plan to use Biosphere 2 to study climate change. Ed Bass donated an additional $30 million to ensure that research at the site continues indefinitely.

The success or failure of the Biosphere 2 experiment may be debated for many years, but one conclusion is certain—Ed Bass' history with Biosphere 2 takes its place securely within, in the words of *Fortune* magazine writer Melanie Warner, "the grand tradition of eccentric American rich guys who use their wealth to pursue quixotic agendas."

Though one may pardon Ed Bass for his possible inadvertent contribution to the advent of reality television, there is one result of this project that is without question inexcusable. Bass' project, sadly, was the inspiration for *Bio-Dome*, a Pauly Shore (ouch!) movie declared by metacritic.com as "the worst movie of all time."

And for that, the world may never forgive Ed Bass.

Chapter 2

"Gradatim Ferociter"

Jeff Bezos
1964-present

Name: Jeffrey Preston Bezos
Lived: 1964-present
Texas connection: Went to elementary school in Houston; owns a West Texas ranch
Occupation: Amazon.com founder and bazillionaire
Claim to weirdness: A private launch pad and the one-and-only Jeff Bezos laugh
Tex-centricity Scale: 4 electronic shopping carts (out of 10)

A Texas eccentric and an air catastrophe; as you read further into this book, you'll find that those two things go together like oil and banking. Or, more befitting our current topic of discussion, like tech fortunes and space tourism.

According to Alan Deutchman in *Fast Company* magazine, Jeff Bezos was in a chartered helicopter in West Texas doing some ranch shopping when a gust of wind blew the chopper's blades into a cedar tree. They have a lot of those in West Texas—cedar trees and gusts of wind. I don't know how many helicopters they have. Anyway, the craft went down into Calamity Creek and Bezos was hospitalized with head lacerations.

Everyone knows who Jeff Bezos is, right? Well, maybe not the Amish—but even they must know what Amazon.com is. After all, if they didn't, how would I be able to buy two pounds of "Amish Country Baby White Popcorn" on that very website for $3.14?

You see my point.

Anyway, even complete Luddites probably have a fleeting notion that the founder of Amazon.com is a youngish billionaire who started the quirky online business in his garage, and who was for some time the dot com poster boy. They may remember that he was named *Time* magazine's Man of the Year in 1999. Some even know that after the dot com bust, he became a favorite target of critics. He took a beating not only in the press, but also financially. In three short years, his net worth plummeted from $10.1 billion in 1999—when he was the 19th richest person in the world—to $1.5 billion in 2002, and the 293rd slot among the richest people in the world. Hard times, indeed.

Not to worry, though. First of all, $1.5 billion isn't all that bad, is it? I mean, don't get me wrong, I have more. But still. Second, Bezos never lost his commitment to the business model of Amazon.com or to the idea of e-commerce as the future of retail. He just kept on doing the same old thing he had been doing—expanding his company and responding to customers' needs. The result? *Forbes* listed him as the 37th richest person in the world in 2007, worth approximately $8.7 billion.

Nice comeback, Jeff.

Most people probably assume that Bezos is a Pacific Northwesterner. Amazon—the company, not the river—is based in Seattle, after all, just up the road from Bill Gates' little software firm. (Salmon go home to mate and geeks go to Washington state.) However, while Bezos may make his home in Washington nowadays, he spent much of his childhood on his grandfather's immense ranch in West Texas. He even spent some time attending elementary school in Houston. Now he's back in Texas, to some extent. That "ranch" he was shopping for—well, there's more to that little story.

But back to the business of Amazon.com for a moment. Why the name Amazon? One story goes that Bezos originally named his site Cadabra (as in abra cadabra), but changed it after a phone conversation in which a friend thought he had said "cadaver." I'm not sure what Bezos has against cadavers, but the reason he renamed the site Amazon was simple: the Amazon moves more water than any river in the world—take that, Nile—and Bezos' website would carry more books than the largest brick and mortar bookstore in the world. The name is perfect in that it meets the number one criteria for naming a major Internet site: complete and unadulterated randomness.

Bezos has not been content to rest on his laurels (or on his giant stacks of cash) as the leader of a billion-dollar business. Unlike the founders of other dot com juggernauts such as eBay, Yahoo, and zFroodle (okay, I made that last one up), Bezos has transitioned from no-name dot com pioneer to seasoned CEO of a *Fortune 500* business. He knows how to start a business, but he also knows how to run one after he gets it started.

One famous and possibly exaggerated story about the beginning of Amazon.com holds that Bezos wrote his business plan in the passenger seat of a Chevy Blazer while his wife drove them from Ft. Worth, Texas, to Seattle, Washington. But the truth is, Bezos didn't exactly start Amazon on a shoestring budget. He had a million dollars in loans from friends and family members with which to start his business.

Since then, Amazon has seen a steady stream of change. It morphed from an online bookstore, plain and simple, to a retailer of all sorts of stuff. It went head-to-head with eBay in the online auction business. It took on added features that allowed it to recommend purchases to its users based on what they've bought in the past and on what others are buying. Later, Bezos surprised many by opening up the groundbreaking code his company had created for other online business ventures, even competitors, to use—he called this new angle Amazon Web Services. Along the way, Bezos also coined the term "artificial artificial intelligence."

After these and about a million other innovations, Jeff Bezos has moved on into space.

Well, he isn't in space yet, but he's getting there. Bezos, as the money behind a company called Blue Origin, has entered the private space race along with fellow computer zillionaires Paul Allen and John Carmack (who is another Texas eccentric, by the way). He now stands alongside hotel magnate Robert Bigelow and Virgin Records mogul Richard Branson, fellow billionaire space pioneers.

Blue Origin has plans to develop a craft that will ferry space tourists to the edge of space. (And back, we hope.) No news on when the first paying flight will occur, but at this writing the www.blueorigin.com website features a video that shows a large white craft, shaped roughly like the nose section of a very fat rocket, successfully lifting off and settling back down vertically in the West Texas desert.

Like Bezos' other, better-known venture, Blue Origin is based in Seattle, but it operates a launch facility built on a 165,000 acre ranch that Bezos purchased outside of Van Horn, Texas. Remember the "ranch shopping" he was doing when his helicopter crapped out and put him in the hospital with boo-boos on his head? Yeah, he was actually out looking for a private space base. Perfectly normal thing for a billionaire to do, I suppose.

But back to Blue Origin. The company's motto is "Gradatim Ferociter," a phrase in Latin that means, roughly, "One step at a time, with spirit." Bezos hopes that his team can create a reliable, reusable, and safe means of travel for those belonging to the money-is-no-object crowd who are interested in experiencing weightlessness and pretending they're John Glenn in *The Right Stuff.*

Bezos is known, obviously, for his willingness to take risks. When he drove across the country to start his new business in Seattle (where he felt he could find plenty of computer programmers to help him), it's important to note what he left behind. After graduating near the top of his class at Princeton with a computer engineering degree, he had landed a job with a million-dollar salary at an investment firm in New York. He walked away from that to start Amazon.

Who walks away from a million dollars?

Jeff Bezos, that's who. He has since said that his reason for walking away from such a promising career had something to do with his "regret minimization framework." (Yep, he really talks like that.) In normal people speech, that means that he didn't want to spend the rest of his life thinking, "What if I had started an online bookstore back before the Internet was big?"

Lucky for him he went through with it, too; because if not, he'd only be a measly millionaire today.

More eccentric than his lack of a risk aversion gene, perhaps, is Jeff Bezos' renowned guffaw. A writer for *MacLean's* describes it this way: "a wheezy blend of whoopee cushion and Pavarotti canto, rising deep from the diaphragm and swallowing the whole room." (Those *MacLean's* people really know how to write.) Another writer says Bezos has "a laugh like a foghorn." Another calls it "a wild, giggly laugh" and still another describes it as an "earthquake."

With $8 billion or so on his personal ledger, Jeff Bezos has a lot to laugh about. And with the independent, git 'er done spirit he developed in part from working on his grandpa's Texas farm back when he was knee-high to a grasshopper, who knows what's to come from this Texas eccentric? Now that he's opened up the Internet as a home to genuine commerce—yes, Amazon.com is turning a profit now—the next boundary he crosses might be the one that leads the common multi-millionaire to the final frontier.

Chapter 3

"Armadillos in Space"

John Carmack
1970-present

Name: John D. Carmack II
Lived: 1970-present
Texas connection: Lives and works in North Central Texas
Occupation: Computer game designer, self-trained rocket scientist
Claim to weirdness: Named his rocket-design firm after a lovable armored varmint
Tex-centricity Scale: 3 Testarossas (out of 10)

Stop me if you've heard this one: eccentric Texas computer genius makes a killing and then uses his riches to enter the space tourism industry.

John D. Carmack II is on the low end of the Tex-centricity Scale (and, like many others in these pages, on the high end of the stinking rich scale). In fact, for a computer nerd, he's almost downright normal, even though Richard Stenger called him "an eccentric Texas technophile" in a 2002 CNN.com article, and even though *Time* magazine labeled him "an odd duck." His eccentric behaviors are limited to quirkiness in conversation, tinkering with a collection of Ferraris, and, most significantly, to turning a childhood hobby—model rocket building—into a very expensive adulthood business that so far hasn't made him a dime.

Unlike some other eccentric Texans, John Carmack didn't inherit a fortune. His father was a television reporter in Kansas City and made a decent living, but he was no mogul. While others took inherited riches and grew them, Carmack built his own wealth practically from scratch.

Like fellow rich guys Jeff Bezos and Sir Richard Branson, John Carmack has entered the 21st century's private space race. This race's ultimate goal is space tourism for the masses, and it was spawned in large part by Peter Diamandis' Ansari X Prize, a $10 million purse offered to the first person or group of private individuals to launch a craft into suborbital spaceflight twice within two weeks. (The prize was claimed in 2004 by Burt Rutan on behalf of Microsoft's Paul Allen—another computer zillionaire with designs on space.)

How did Carmack make his money? Well, he only developed the best-selling computer game franchise of all time: *Doom*. Add to that other notable titles like *Castle Wolfenstein* and *Quake* and you end up with a very rich man. Carmack is widely known in game development circles as a virtuosic genius when it comes to building gaming engines. Gamers on their geeky forums have extolled him as a "pioneer," a "wizard," and an "eccentric uber-coding monkey Godness," whatever that means. Cyberfight.org calls him "John 'The God' Carmack." *Time* magazine listed him at number 10 on their "Digital 50" list.

So, yeah, he's a pretty big deal.

But he's also a little weird.

Despite his near-divine programming abilities and his heroic status among a seriously oddball populace, Carmack leads a relatively normal family life in Dallas, Texas. At some point along the way, he realized that he was spending more money tinkering with his Ferraris than it would take to build a working rocket, so he assembled a team to do just that.

At this point I shall prove that Mr. Carmack does indeed belong in these eccentric pages of Texas, for Carmack named his high-fallutin' space age venture not Orion Enterprises nor Horizons Incorporated, but...are you ready for this?

Armadillo Aerospace.

That's right, he named it after Texas' famed (and, I might add, flightless) armor-plated highway rat, that precocious little ball of leprosy that jumps exactly bumper-high when frightened by oncoming headlights; that cute creature we've all seen laying dead on its back with a Lone Star beer bottle clenched between its hairy claws.

Ten years from now, when a space tourist is strapped to one of Carmack's giant tubes of highly explosive material and is hurtling through the atmosphere and possibly thinking about space disasters like Apollo, Challenger, and Columbia, he'll be in a craft built by people who were inspired by the lowly armadillo. I can't think of anything that would make him or her feel more at ease.

No one is completely sure why Carmack so named his company, but the Armadillo Aerospace website says the name was chosen for its "local flavor." We can conclude, then, that John Carmack eats armadillos. I actually thought the name had something to do with the aerodynamic shape of the little buggers, but I guess I was wrong. It happens. (Just ask my wife.)

While Carmack and his team chose a quirky name for their company, the work they do is completely serious. Having competed in the Ansari X Prize competition and the Northrup

Grumman Lunar Lander Challenge, their current plans are to compete and win in other big-name rocketry and space-related contests. The company's ultimate goal is to create cheap access to space, something NASA has been thus far unable or unwilling to accomplish.

Carmack isn't just throwing his money away, either. He sees a "really significant business opportunity" in space tourism, noting in an interview with CNET News that Virgin Spaceways has already banked $20 million in deposits for eventual low-orbit spaceflights. Carmack sees lucrative opportunities, as well, in "vertical drag racing" (two rockets go up; first one to the finish line wins) and in recreational space diving (like sky diving but, you know, from space).

Despite his foray into the modern space race, Carmack has continued to produce eagerly-awaited games from the offices of id Software in Dallas. While the video game thing pays his bills, if Carmack has his way, there'll be more money to be made soon. He believes, according to the 2006 CNET interview, that people will be punching their tickets to space within the next 10 years.

In the end, this author isn't sure if that makes him eccentric, or just audacious enough to make another fortune.

Chapter 4

"Generous to a Fault"

Edgar Byram Davis
1873-1951

Name: Edgar Byram Davis
Lived: 1873-1951
Texas connection: Made a fortune in Luling, Texas
Occupation: Shoe, rubber, and oil magnate
Claim to weirdness: Single-handedly kept the worst play in Broadway going for 2 years
Tex-centricity Scale: 7 Tony Awards (out of 10)

Edgar Byram Davis made his first million dollars in the state where he was born, Massachusetts, as owner of the Walkover shoe company. He made his next three million as a major investor in one of the first rubber firms to do business in the US.

In the early 1920s, Davis, already rich, followed his brother to Caldwell County, Texas, and invested with him in the hunt for black gold. In a gesture of solidarity with the locals, he named his new company "United North and South Oil Company, Inc." and then proceeded to drill six dry holes. An inveterate mystic, Davis eventually consulted a friend who had gotten a hot tip on oil formations from psychic Edgar Cayce. Davis finally hit pay dirt in the Luling field in 1922 and made his third fortune.

One historian tells it this way:

> [A] depressed if not totally discouraged group of three United North and South people, Edgar Davis, Agnes Manford and W. F. Peale, sat watching the hypnotic rotary grinding away at 2,100 feet. Just as Peale, at the wheel of their car, was about to drive away, Miss Manford is reported to have pointed and shouted (in a most undignified way): "Look, Boys, Look!"

According to the account, the car Davis and his friends sat in was promptly soaked with oil from the gusher and Davis, instead of taking the car to the carwash, insisted that they immediately drive it into the town of Luling and stop at Mackey's Drug Store, a store owned (obviously) by one Mr. Mackey, a local who had publicly ridiculed Davis' search for oil in a place geologists had said held no oil.

Davis was a deeply religious man, albeit in an unconventional way. He had been spiritually impacted during a rubber-related trip to Sumatra. A *Time* article from 1928 stated that "In the Orient, Edgar B. Davis, U. S. businessman, became Edgar B. Davis, mystic. Eastern religion had touched his imagination; mysticism satisfied his soul."

Davis always wrote the word FAITH in all caps, he believed in reincarnation, and, while he belonged to no church, he regularly attended all the churches in Luling. In fact, Davis moved south from Massachusetts specifically because he "believed that he was directed by God to come to Texas and to deliver Luling and Caldwell County from the oppressive one-crop (cotton) economy that dominated the area."

Davis was also a very generous man—inordinately so, his heirs might say. When he earned $12 million for the sale of his holdings at Luling, he held a huge barbecue for friends and associates. According to one source, 15,000 to 35,000 people showed up. He also gave his employees bonuses ranging from 25 to 100 percent of their annual salaries. The total layout for this expression of gratitude was in the range of $1 million. In addition, he built a variety of facilities for the people of Luling and established the Luling Foundation for the teaching of better agricultural methods. It still exists today.

Davis also funded a series of art competitions that were "among the most significant cultural events in Texas during those formative years of the twentieth century." In addition, he bailed out Frank A. Seiberling, a former president of Goodyear Tire and Rubber Company. *Time* reports the story this way:

> In 1920 the business depression which jostled William Crapo Durant out of General Motors jolted Frank A. Seiberling out of Goodyear. He retained his stock in the corporation, but had no money. As many men did, Edgar B. Davis knew of the wreckage; as few men did, he went to Mr. Seiberling's help. Together they formed the Prudential Securities Co. Mr. Davis put in $500,000 and guaranteed $5,000,000 of company pledges. To the Prudential Securities Co. Mr. Seiberling pledged his Goodyear stock and other personal assets, and thereby secured cash. Friend Davis in a corporate way had loaned the money.
>
> That cash helped finance the Seiberling Rubber Co. six years ago. President Frank A. Seiberling of Seiberling Rubber (his second great rubber company)

has made it successful, prosperous. For 1927 its net profits were $1,356,707.

With the "comeback" of the rubber industry, Prudential Securities has made money on the Goodyear and Seiberling rubber company stocks, which it held. But Prudential Securities was created to help Mr. Seiberling, not to profit. Therefore, slight Mr. Seiberling and bulky Mr. Davis met in the Cleveland lawyers' office last week and dissolved the company. This relieved Mr. Davis of his $5,000,000 guarantee and it repaid him his $500,000 cash. Mr. Seiberling and lawyers tried to persuade him to accept interest on his money. He refused. Said he: "Business is business, but friendship is also friendship."

The most telling example of Davis' eccentricity and generosity involves a play, *The Ladder*, written by a friend, one James Francis Davis (no relation). Historians note that, because he approved of its message of reincarnation, Edgar Byram Davis paid to produce the show and keep it going for two years, making it (at that time) the fourth-longest running play in Broadway history. The play was not a success and, in order to keep it going, Davis resorted to purchasing the tickets himself and having them given away to incredulous Manhattanites. *Time*, in announcing his death in 1951, noted that Davis "squandered $1,300,000 on it [*The Ladder*] before it closed in 1927 to the faint applause of 54 nonpaying guests."

Davis' liberality knew no bounds. He was convinced that his wealth was meant for the greater good of mankind, and the author of "Oil and Texas: A Cultural History" notes that Davis "gave away so much money that he was almost broke when he died."

This fact alone makes him one of the nicest millionaires in Texas history, but also one of the most eccentric.

Chapter 5

"Lord British"

Richard Garriott
1961-present

Name: Richard Allen Garriott
Lived: 1961-present
Texas connection: Raised in Nassau Bay, Texas; resides in Austin
Occupation: Computer game designer; space tourist
Claim to weirdness: Lives in a castle; paid big bucks for a trip to the International Space Station
Tex-centricity Scale: 6 secret passageways (out of 10)

Richard Garriott picked up the nickname "Lord British" in high school because older classmates thought he spoke with a British accent. No word on how many times he had his butt kicked by jocks who didn't like his Queen's English. Meanwhile, he has since retained the appellation for use in online game play. Interestingly, unlike other people who come up with snazzy names for their online characters, Garriott actually designed the games he plays as Lord British.

I first learned of Richard Garriott while watching a television documentary about interesting houses in America. While I don't remember the name of the show, I do remember his house: Brittania Manor (again with the British thing). Britannia Manor is a giant castle just outside of Austin that comes complete with suits of armor, crossbows, an honest-to-goodness vampire-hunting kit, an actual human skeleton in an actual casket, and even a working observatory. I remember watching Garriott show off the numerous secret passageways and trapdoors in his home. Garriott had spent untold dollars on his anachronistic manor in Austin, and he told the reporter that he had plans to build an even larger one.

Like fellow Texas eccentric John Carmack, Garriott is a young millionaire who made his fortune designing video games. As founder of Origin Systems, some of the titles Garriott has produced include *Ultima I* through *IX*, *Bioforge*, *Lineage*, *City of Heroes*, and *Tabula Rasa*. All told, he has had a hand in the development of dozens of very popular games. And to think, he sold his first games on floppy disks in Ziploc bags to schoolmates.

Also like Carmack, Garriott has an abiding interest in space tourism. He is a trustee for the X Prize organization and is on the board of directors for industry pioneer Space Adventures. While Carmack spends his money developing rockets, though, Garriott has opted for a role as passenger. He spent "at least $30 million" for an October 2008 flight to the International Space Station aboard a Soyuz rocket. Unlike other millionaire space tourists, though, Richard Garriott has a prior connection to space. His scientist father spent 59 days in orbit over the earth in Skylab and returned to space ten years later aboard the Columbia space shuttle.

Richard Garriott was born in Cambridge, England, to

American parents. He took an interest in computer programming in high school. He sold his first game to an actual company in 1980 and used the proceeds to pay for tuition at the University of Texas at Austin. While there, he displayed flashes of the eccentricity that would later define him: he joined the fencing team and, appropriately for a fan of all things archaic, joined the Society for Creative Anachronism. (He was in it for the chicks.)

Richard Garriott, like other computer millionaires, is a model of what happens when a nerd gets fabulously wealthy. Perhaps excessive wealth doesn't change a person, but only exaggerates his or her inborn traits. A mean man made rich may become unbearable. A controlling man may become a tyrant. However, nerds made rich will do things like pay to ride in rockets, live in castles, or spend their lives designing and playing MMORPGs (that's "massively multi-player online role-playing games," for those of you who aren't in the know).

Eccentric, yes. But it doesn't sound like such a bad way to live. If you had Garriott's money, you'd probably do some oddball things yourself.

Chapter 6

"King of the Texas Eccentrics"

Howard Hughes
1905-1976

Name: Howard Robard Hughes, Jr.
Lived: 1905-1976
Texas connection: Born in Houston or Humble (depending on who you ask)
Occupation: Industrialist, aviation entrepreneur, national hero, and movie maker
Claim to weirdness: Germophobe, hermit, pea sorter, and pee hoarder
Tex-centricity Scale: 10 giant wooden airplanes (out of 10)

Thanks to the popular 2004 Leonardo DiCaprio film *The Aviator*—and also to the high profile roles he filled during his lifetime as a movie mogul, a record-setting aviation pioneer, a Congressional Medal of Honor winner, and a billionaire when billionaires were unheard of—Howard Hughes is possibly the most universally recognizable eccentric listed in these pages. Raised by a mother some have posthumously labeled obsessive-compulsive (she refused to let him go to summer camp because of polio fears and she kept him out of school frequently, fearing germs), Howard likely inherited his quirks from her. He struggled with tics and obsessive behaviors all his life. But Hughes wasn't just odd—he skirted the line between mere eccentricity and downright weirdness for most of his life.

Howard Hughes' father, a Texas wildcatter, invented the triple-cone rotary drill bit for drilling oil wells when little Howard was only four years old. Howard, Sr., founded Hughes Tool Company to market his invention, and then he started buying up the patents of other drill bits and invented still others. Soon, Hughes owned a successful company and Howard Robard Hughes, Jr., became a child of wealth and privilege.

After his mother's death from complications during pregnancy (she lost the baby and Howard remained an only child) and his father's death shortly thereafter from a heart attack, Junior inherited most of the family fortune at the ripe old age of 19. The year was 1925. He had been captivated a couple of years earlier when his father took him to Hollywood, and after he got his hands on the family fortune he immediately relocated to California to try his hand in the movie business. Within three years, Howard Hughes the younger had made three movies, one of which, 1928's comedy *Two Arabian Knights,* won an Academy Award.

In 1930, Hughes began production on *Hell's Angels,* a ground-breaking film about something Howard had loved since childhood—airplanes. He had taken his first flying lessons at age 14 and had been enamored of all things mechanical from his earliest years.

To make *Hell's Angels,* the millionaire-soon-to-be-billionaire ended up buying an entire fleet of aircraft with his own money. To make it perfect, he directed the dogfights himself. He was forced to reshoot a significant portion of the film and replace the foreign lead actress with an American when it became apparent that silent films were no longer popular. By the end of production, *Hell's Angels* was the most expensive movie ever made. Despite cost overruns and delays in its release, it was received warmly by audiences and became a box office smash.

In spite of his success in the movie business, Howard never forgot his first love. He started Hughes Aircraft Company as a division of Hughes Tool Company while living in California and soon began building airplanes that he himself would pilot to glory. Howard Hughes set one aviation record after another during the 1930s. He set the airspeed record in 1935; the transcontinental airspeed record in 1937; the speed record for flying around the world in 1938. These record-breaking flights propelled Hughes to national fame. Soon, he was considered an American hero. He was awarded the Congressional Medal of Honor in 1939.

The most famous flying creation of Hughes Aircraft Company was the so-called "Spruce Goose," a derisive name for the Hughes H-4 Hercules, which was actually made of birch. The Hercules had a larger wingspan than anything before or since. It was made of wood because the military contract that called for it specified that it not be made out of "strategic materials," things like steel and aluminum. Hughes and his associates endured great criticism during the building of the audacious wooden monster, criticism reminiscent of that which greeted the making of his movie *Hell's Angels.* Many thought the plane, larger than any ever built before, would never fly. Despite the criticism, Hughes presented the completed H-4 Hercules to the U.S. government in 1947; it flew once for 60 seconds, with Hughes himself at the helm.

A congressional inquiry was launched soon after the sale regarding the lateness of Hughes Aircraft in supplying the plane. This would not be the last time Hughes found himself entangled with the government.

A year before the completion of the H-4 Hercules, Hughes almost died when he crashed an experimental spy plane he was test piloting for the U.S. Army. Hughes suffered severe burns and dozens of broken bones in the crash, and many historians attribute later problems Hughes had with controlled substances to his use of opiates during his recovery from this accident.

Hughes' ties to aviation went beyond setting records as a pilot and building airplanes. In 1939, he bought enough stock to gain majority control of Trans-World Airlines. From early on, Hughes sought to use his money and influence to control outside events regarding his business interests. So when Senator Owen Brewster proposed legislation that would have made Pan American World Airways the only American airline allowed to fly overseas, Hughes used his considerable resources to uncover influence-peddling in the case and then spent a significant amount to ensure that Senator Bennett's opponent defeated him when it was time for re-election.

He gave up his personal residence and chose instead to move from hotel to hotel every five and a half months to avoid taxes.

Political involvement was a key strategy that Hughes employed to achieve his desired ends; this often meant making donations to candidates. Some historians contend that Hughes was, in a roundabout way, responsible for Richard Nixon's Watergate scandal. He had made a $100,000 payment to Nixon confidant Bebe Rebozo, and some inside the administration have since said that Nixon ordered the hotel break-in to find out if the Democrats knew about it.

This theory has never been confirmed, but what is certain is that Hughes was very active in trying to manipulate political events using his wealth. When he lived in Las Vegas, for example, he tried unsuccessfully to stop underground nuclear testing nearby—he was concerned about radiation poisoning—

going so far as to instruct his handlers to offer million dollar bribes to two sitting Presidents.

Radiation poisoning was not the only contamination that concerned Hughes. From childhood he was conscious of the danger of germs, and a mild fear grew into a major phobia as he grew older. He conducted most of his business over the phone and through written memos in order to avoid contamination from the people he worked with. Though this and other quirks were manifest from childhood—he was paralyzed for months in 1919, for unknown reasons—they became more and more of an impairment as he grew older.

Many today point to symptoms of obsessive-compulsive disorder evident in Hughes' later life. For example, he became obsessed with the size of peas and sorted them before eating. He stopped trimming his hair and nails and brushing his teeth. He wore tissue boxes on his feet near the end of his life, and he kept his urine in jars in his closet. He once piloted a small plane over London—in the nude.

It should be noted that Hughes never received any sort of medical attention for his mental state—he was undiagnosed during his lifetime. Back then, they had another word for obsessive-compulsive disorder. They called it "crazy." They used this same handy medical term to describe attention deficit disorder, multiple personality disorder, schizophrenia, oppositional defiant disorder, and many others. Fortunately, psychologists in the latter half of the 20th century discovered that really long words and phrases that can be converted into acronyms make better names for screwy brain problems.

His fragile mental condition was almost certainly worsened by his long-running addiction to codeine, as well as from a possible case of neurosyphilis resulting from an apparent contraction of syphilis as a young man. Some historians even conjecture that he may have suffered brain damage from any or all of the four airplane crashes he was in during his lifetime.

By the end of his life, Hughes lived in almost total

seclusion. He surrounded himself with a group of Mormon advisers. He wasn't a Mormon, but he trusted Latter-Day Saints to be honest with his money. He moved from hotel to hotel, staying in London, Vancouver, Managua, and Acapulco, among other places. His second wife claimed she went years without seeing or hearing from him, and few people knew where he was staying at any given time. He made a brief "appearance" in 1971, albeit only by telephone, to refute a fake autobiography of him that a fraudster named Clifford Irving had sold to McGraw-Hill for $750,000; and then he disappeared again.

In 1976, Howard Hughes was flown from Acapulco, Mexico, to a hospital in Houston for medical attention. He had survived multiple plane crashes during his lifetime, but, ironically, he died in the air on this flight. When his body arrived back home to Texas, he was unrecognizable. His emaciated, toothless, drug-riddled body, complete with several needle tips imbedded under his skin, had to be identified through fingerprint analysis.

During his lifetime, Howard Hughes was not accustomed to finishing second in anything. His unbending obsession with being the best made him the richest man in the world, a national aviation hero, and a movie mogul without equal. He founded the Howard Hughes Medical Institute, which today is still a major research foundation. The same quality that drove him to the top perhaps also drove him over the edge. It is appropriate, then, that this giant among men also takes his place as a giant among eccentric Texans.

Chapter 7

"Twice the Marital Bliss"

H. L. Hunt
1889-1974

Name: Haroldson Lafayette Hunt, Jr.
Lived: 1889-1974
Texas connection: Lived in Dallas
Occupation: Oilman, investor, food and cosmetic entrepreneur
Claim to weirdness: Liked wives so much, he kept two at a time
Tex-centricity Scale: 7 wedding bands (out of 10)

Haroldson Lafayette Hunt, Jr., born in Illinois, came to Texas after making a good deal of money investing an inheritance of $6000 in cotton plantations and then in oil patches in Arkansas. By the time he left Arkansas, he was worth an estimated $600,000.

In 1930, Hunt engineered a deal with a man named C. M.

"Dad" Joiner, a wildcatter in East Texas. Joiner was in a pinch. He had discovered oil on his 4000 acre place but didn't have enough money to drill. Banks wouldn't loan him the money, and other oilmen were stung from the market crash of 1929. In stepped H. L. Hunt. He offered Joiner $30,000 and a promise of more if and when they hit oil.

And hit oil they did, in a big way. The East Texas oilfield was the largest deposit of oil discovered to that date. Soon, Hunt was building his own pipelines to supply Standard Oil Company.

The Handbook of Texas Online notes that Hunt was eventually considered the richest man in the nation: "On April 5, 1948, *Fortune* printed a story on Hunt that labeled him the richest man in the United States." Many historians contend that Hunt was also the richest man in the world late in his life.

H. L. Hunt's eccentricity shone through in several areas of his life. The first was marriage. Infidelity in the marriage of a mogul is probably not all that unusual, but H. L. Hunt married one Frania Tye of Florida while he was still married to the former Ms. Lyda Bunker of Arkansas. Bigamy—now you don't see that everyday. Hunt kept his two growing families in two different cities, maintaining both and traveling back and forth for some seventeen years. Between the two wives, Hunt fathered 10 children. The charade lasted until he became a well-known figure. Frania figured out what was going on in the early 1940s and H. L. Hunt was forced to set up trusts for the four children he had with her, to pledge financial support for her, and to dissolve the relationship. When Lyda died in 1955, H. L. Hunt married another woman, his secretary, with whom he already had four children.

The second area of oddness was found in the exaggerated unpretentiousness Hunt displayed in his daily life. Despite his world-class wealth, he lived in a modest home in Dallas and mowed his own grass once a week. One biographer notes that H. L. Hunt carried his lunch to work in a brown paper bag every day. Yet, despite this apparent humility, Hunt was known to introduce himself to strangers by telling them right away that he was the richest man in the world.

In his later years, Hunt entered the world of politics, focusing his efforts on conservative political commentary, financing radio and television programs and writing a newspaper column to promote his ideas. He supported Joseph McCarthy's movement to root out communists from American society. He supported Barry Goldwater for President in 1964 and was a member of the ultra-conservative John Birch Society. Nevertheless, he donated money and lobbied for a variety of candidates for public office, including liberals like John F. Kennedy and Lyndon Baines Johnson. Hunt withdrew his support from Kennedy, however, after his administration didn't go the way Hunt wanted on an issue involving oil revenue.

Finally, Hunt's lone foray into literature revealed a sliver of his oddball streak. He self-published a utopian novel, *Alpaca*, and distributed it to dozens of world leaders. An article about the rare book in the *Dallas Business Journal* described it as the story of Juan Achala, a young man who left his home in the nation of Alpaca and searched the world for a cure for dictatorship. After talking to several prominent folks the world over, Achala came up with a perfect constitution, one that would make dictatorship impossible. Hunt included a copy of the perfect constitution in the appendix of the novel. World leaders, according to the article, were polite, but none of them adopted Hunt's constitution for their countries.

His lifetime ended over three decades ago, but H. L. Hunt's 15 children have continued in his footsteps, demonstrating business acumen as well as occasionally strange behavior. In the most well-known case of the latter (and definitely not the former) his son Bunker once led a family attempt to corner the world silver market. The attempt failed, shook the silver market and the stock market, and caused the family to lose hundreds of millions of dollars. Other business ventures have fared better, however, and the Hunt family continues to wield great influence in the state of Texas.

Chapter 8

"The Charismatic Leader"

Herb Kelleher
1931-present

Name: Herbert D. Kelleher
Lived: 1931-present
Texas connection: Lived in San Antonio and currently lives in Dallas
Occupation: Former CEO of Southwest Airlines
Claim to weirdness: Once arm-wrestled another CEO for use of a slogan
Tex-centricity Scale: 6 bags of peanuts (out of 10)

Herb Kelleher forged a name for himself as a fun-loving, eccentric chief and, in the meantime, created a very successful business. While other airlines around the country floundered, Southwest Airlines consistently turned a tidy profit. Kelleher and his team pulled this off by keeping costs low—they served peanuts instead of meals on their flights, and they flew into secondary airports. Many times over, Southwest was voted one of America's "Best Places to Work." Kelleher's leadership style combined light-hearted antics with serious business and notwithstanding a hefty fine for missed inspections in 2008, Southwest has consistently had one of the nation's best safety records since its beginning.

Kelleher's antics are the stuff of legend. He has dressed up like Elvis, like a leprechaun, and like the Easter Bunny. He has "jumped out of overhead bins." While other big shot CEOs drove (or were driven, perhaps) to work in sober luxury sedans, Kelleher's vehicle of choice for a time was a motorcycle that had been gifted to him by his pilots.

Kelleher's colorful style trickled down and resulted in a company culture noted for zaniness. Flight attendants sometimes sang their in-flight announcements, for example. Employees loved their jobs, and Kelleher was something of a hero to his employees.

Perhaps the most famous of Kelleher's stunts involved an arm-wrestling match with the CEO of another airline. The PBS website describes the incident in this way:

> One outrageous incident was his arm-wrestling showdown with the CEO of Stevens Aviation in 1992. Both Stevens and Southwest were using the advertising tagline "Plane Smart." To settle the matter, Kelleher suggested an arm-wrestling competition with the winner keeping the rights to the slogan. Kelleher lost the match, but the event generated so much good will and publicity that Stevens let Southwest continue use of the tagline.

Kelleher's unconventional approach to business resulted in more than just a successful enterprise. Kelleher earned for himself the undying respect and admiration of his employees, whom he always treated with respect, and whom he trusted to do their jobs well. Kelleher proved that you can have fun and be successful in business, and do both at the same time. He showed the rest of the world the right way to run a business.

Even if he did dress like Elvis from time to time.

Chapter 9

"The Cadillac Rancher"

Stanley Marsh 3
c. 1938-present

Name: Stanley Marsh 3
Lived: c. 1938-present
Texas connection: Lives in Amarillo
Occupation: Artist, philanthropist, television station owner
Claim to weirdness: Responsible for a several odd works of "art" in and around Amarillo
Tex-centricity Scale: 10 half-buried Cadillacs (out of 10)

Stanley Marsh 3 is a millionaire businessman from Amarillo, Texas. He's the grandson of legendary Texas oilman Stanley Marsh and ranks among the oddest of the oddball characters that the Lone Star State has yet produced. An avid supporter of the arts, Marsh is responsible for a variety of public art projects (also known as "eyesores" to some locals) in and around the West Texas hamlet of Amarillo.

The most famous of Stanley Marsh's weird projects is the so-called "Cadillac Ranch," a display of ten 1950s-era Cadillacs buried nose first in a field beside Interstate 40. The art display is decidedly "hands on"—the public is invited to climb on the cars and even to vandalize them with spray paint. Other public art projects include "Dynamite Museum," a collection of hundreds of fake road signs scattered around Amarillo and nearby Adrian, Texas, with humorous or nonsensical sayings on them. The first sign erected reads: "Road Does Not End." Other sayings on Marsh's signs include: "If you took everyone who fell asleep in church and put them end to end in a line on the floor they'd be much more comfortable;" "Lubbock is a grease spot;" "Bob at our cherries, bite at our peaches;" and "I'll be right out, Ma! For crying out loud." Some merely bear pictures, like the sign depicting Marilyn Monroe, placed (appropriately enough) alongside Monroe Street.

Marsh originally placed his fake signs on the public right-of-way. When he was informed that this was against the law, he started placing them on private property, with the consent of property owners.

Marsh has also commissioned a pair of disembodied legs standing in an open field. This work was based on lines two and three of the Percy Bysshe Shelley poem "Ozymandias," which say, "two vast and trunkless legs of stone/Stand in the desert..." In addition, Marsh has a giant pool table visible only from the air hidden somewhere on the thousands of acres he owns. He also commissioned a project in which countless sheets of plywood were nailed together and painted white to create a strip just below the top of a mesa. The title of that work is "Floating Mesa" and the white band is supposed to give the impression that the top of the mesa is floating in the sky. The only problem is that the optical illusion only works when the sky is just the right shade of white, which it never is.

Stanley Marsh is (as far as we know) the only person in this book who has inspired two different folk songs. Bruce Springsteen wrote a song titled "Cadillac Ranch," as did folk singer John Stewart.

Stanley Marsh is widely quoted as having said, "Art is a legalized form of insanity, and I do it very well." But his eccentricity isn't limited to his taste in art and his willingness to spend money on gaudy displays of it, or to his unwillingness to use the traditional "III" at the end of his name, claiming it less pretentious to use the Arabic numeral "3."

No, the millionaire's bizarre behavior goes beyond that, extending even into the courtroom. In 2001, he settled four civil lawsuits with a public apology and other undisclosed terms.

The first of the lawsuits stemmed from an episode in which Marsh allegedly locked a teenager inside a chicken coop. The teen had apparently vandalized one of Marsh's mock street signs, and he just happened to belong to the prominent Whittenburg family. Like the Marshes, they were an oil and gas dynasty in Amarillo, and, according to Marsh, co-participants with his family in a long-running feud.

The second lawsuit arose after Marsh allegedly threatened two local teens who had stolen one of his signs. According to the *Amarillo Globe-News*, he told the boys that he would run their names on his television station as thieves unless they spent a day working for him on his property. The boys claimed that their workday ended with an episode of cruel and unusual punishment—Marsh reading poetry to them.

Another case revolved around one Jodi Parker, an Amarillo resident who said she was terrorized when Marsh and his oddball cronies showed up at her house in clown wigs and Lone Ranger masks looking for her stepbrother.

In 1999, in another widely-publicized event, Marsh and three "young people" interrupted a live broadcast of the Weather Channel in Amarillo by doing a "Quanah Parker snow dance" to the blaring sounds of the *Star Wars* theme song, as the reporter tried to file his report. After asking Marsh to leave repeatedly, the reporter finally had to cancel his report. Marsh only left after the police were called.

"I have a constitutional right to do a snow dance," Marsh said later. "I didn't hurt anyone. I was just doing what I always do."

Marsh has been featured in a documentary, *Road Does Not End*, produced and directed by independent filmmaker Todd Kent, and also in the award-winning *The Plutonium Circus*, a film about the United States' only nuclear weapons assembly and disassembly plant in Amarillo, and the "zany folks that live and work in and around it." (No word as to whether the people who came up with this line meant to imply that people live inside the nuclear plant.)

But back to Marsh. Stanley Marsh 3 claims he doesn't see himself as an eccentric. But, with his buried Cadillacs, nonsensical street signs, and generally bizarre behavior, he may very well be the only one who doesn't.

Chapter 10

"What's in a Name?"

Samuel Maverick
1803-1870

Name: Samuel Augustus Maverick
Lived: 1803-1870
Texas connection: Lived in San Antonio and Matagorda Bay, Texas
Occupation: Land speculator, cattleman, and Texas state congressman
Claim to weirdness: Refused to mark his cattle with a brand
Tex-centricity Scale: 2 branding irons (out of 10)

Samuel Augustus Maverick is one of many Texas characters whose story could fit into various sections in this book. He was a politician as well as a businessman in early Texas history. He takes his place in this chapter because his eccentricity came through more in his activities as a businessman than as a politician. That isn't to say that he wasn't an important political figure in his lifetime. In fact, Maverick (not to be confused with Samuel Maverick the American colonist) was a key political player in Texas under four different flags—the Mexican flag, the Republic of Texas flag, the US flag, and the flag of the Confederate States of America.

Maverick's father was a successful businessman in South Carolina. Maverick the younger studied at Yale and became a lawyer in South Carolina. He ran unsuccessfully for a seat in that state's legislature (the loss due primarily to his anti-secessionist views) before moving to Alabama to run a plantation his father owned. Not long after he arrived in Alabama, however, Samuel Maverick chose to move to Texas and try his hand at land speculation.

Land in Texas was plentiful and cheap. Unfortunately, there were tensions brewing between the Anglo settlers and the Mexican government. And there were Indian problems, too.

You get what you pay for when you buy cheap land, I guess.

Anyway, Maverick walked right into a brewing storm in 1835 and soon found himself under house arrest in San Antonio, which was under siege by Texians. When he was freed, he immediately found the Anglo raiders and assisted them. After the successful siege, he was elected delegate to an Independence Convention. In 1839, after a few years spent back in Alabama getting married and helping with his father's business, Maverick was elected mayor of San Antonio. Along with many others, he fled San Antonio in 1842, fearing a Mexican invasion. He returned not long after for the fall term of district court—he served as a judge as well as mayor—and was taken prisoner by Mexican general Adrián Woll. In 1843, under pressure from the U.S. government, Woll released him from prison and Maverick returned to San Antonio to serve in the Congress of the Republic of Texas. As a congressman for the Republic, Maverick steadfastly pressed for annexation into the United States.

Maverick served six terms as a Democrat in the state legislature after Texas joined the United States, spending his time and energy pushing for equal rights for German and Mexican immigrants and fighting against the move toward secession. When it became obvious that secession was going to happen, he joined the Confederate cause and was appointed a secession commissioner for the Texas Secession Convention. He served in a variety of local political posts during the Civil War, including a second term as mayor of San Antonio. After the war, he was pardoned and spent the rest of his life fighting against the rise of radical Republicanism in the state during Reconstruction.

Maverick steadily increased his land holdings throughout his lifetime. By the time he died, he owned over 300,000 acres, most of it in West Texas, where a county is named for him today. A small amount of the land he owned was located on Matagorda Peninsula, where he placed a herd of 400 cattle he had received as payment for a debt. Unlike practically every other cattle rancher in the country at that time, Maverick never branded the offspring of this herd and he let them run wild on the peninsula. In 1854, Maverick drove the cattle closer to San Antonio and continued allowing them to wander free and unbranded. Pretty soon, cattlemen in the area knew that if they found an unbranded heifer, it was "one of Maverick's." The term "maverick" soon came to mean two things: an unbranded calf and an independent individual, someone who does things his own way.

Sam Maverick did indeed do things his own way. A successful man in business and politics, he constantly bucked the trends of his day. And perhaps that maverick spirit is what lured him to Texas in the first place. It takes a different kind of person to uproot and leave a settled land for a wide open place like Texas in the 1830s, a place full of wild Indians and caught in the midst of a quarrel between the Mexican government and a bunch of rabble rousers.

It takes an independent spirit to step into that kind of tinderbox for the promise of cheap land, and that's just what men like Maverick, Sam Houston, and the heroes of the Alamo did. And maybe that's one reason why we have so many eccentrics in Texas today—these men left behind their wild and woolly genes, and their wild and woolly examples.

Chapter 11

"The Shampoo King"

John McCall
1947-present

Name: John Herschel McCall
Lived: 1947-present
Texas connection: "The Shampoo King from Dripping
Springs"
Occupation: Owner of Armstrong McCall, a major beauty
supply distributor
Claim to weirdness: Spent $850,000 on Kinky Friedman's
2006 gubernatorial campaign
Tex-centricity Scale: 9 straightening irons (out of 10)

John McCall is not only a friend and political supporter of
Kinky Friedman, he's also a regular character in Friedman's
fiction. And like Kinky, John McCall is a verifiable Texas
eccentric, an irreverent soul with a taste for humor and a

cockeyed way of looking at the world.

In an interview with the *Austin American-Statesman*, McCall said he described himself as a "Baptist-Buddhist" because Buddhists "have those little statues that people leave money in." In another strange-ish move, McCall gave filmmaker Ellen Spiro a houseboat in exchange for her making a documentary about him, 1999's *The Shampoo King*. He also once owned a spacious mansion he called the "Taj McCall," on the outskirts of Austin.

McCall is such good friends with Friedman that he donated $850,000 to the latter's gubernatorial campaign. Friedman said that voters didn't have to worry about him being in McCall's pocket because McCall was "richer than God" and didn't need anything from the state of Texas.

In *The Shampoo King*, Ellen Spiro compares McCall to the protagonist of American movie masterpiece *Citizen Kane*, news magnate John Foster Kane. Writing for the *Austin American-Statesman*, Sidney Moody notes that both men "inherited a business in their twenties and expanded them far beyond the visions of the founders, both built huge mansions, and both collect artifacts from all corners of the planet....McCall even bears a slight resemblance to Orson Welles."

The parallels between McCall and other Texas eccentrics are surprising. Like Howard Hughes and Tom Slick, he inherited a small fortune and turned it into a large one. He also survived a plane crash—Hughes survived four of them, and Slick survived one and died in another. Likewise, McCall used his wealth to pursue his own quixotic ends. Some might say that Tom Slick's expensive pursuit of Bigfoot had a better likelihood of finding success than McCall's expensive pursuit of the governorship for his friend. Also, like any number of Texas' eccentric millionaires (although, to be accurate, Friedman calls McCall a "centimillionaire" because he doesn't have mere millions, but hundreds of millions), McCall has travelled the world and lived the life of a true jetsetter.

McCall's life is about more than just his wealth and his friendship with Kinky Friedman, however. Throughout his lifetime, he has demonstrated personal qualities such as generosity and an amazing resilience in the face of difficulty. He isn't just an eccentric; he's an eccentric with courage and a generous spirit. His business fell apart in 1984 and he brought it back, in Kinky Friedman's words, "bigger than ever." He has fought cancer twice and won. And along the way, he has donated millions to a variety of charities, usually anonymously.

John McCall is the type of Texas eccentric who seems to embrace the role. According to Moody in the *American-Statesman*, McCall is "more like a fictional character than a real, live person." Maybe that's why Kinky Friedman keeps using him in his novels.

Chapter 12

"He Won't Sell a Fat, Yella Chicken"

Bo Pilgrim
?-present

Name: Lonnie Pilgrim
Lived: ?-present
Texas connection: Grew up and lives in Pittsburg, Texas
Occupation: Chick magnate
Claim to weirdness: The giant statue of his head in downtown Pittsburg
Tex-centricity Scale: 6 drumsticks (out of 10)

Bo Pilgrim has a big head. I don't mean he's arrogant—by all accounts, he's a humble, dedicated Baptist. But he does have a huge head. It sits atop a pavilion in his hometown of Pittsburg, underneath an equally gigantic pilgrim hat (the kind of black, wide-rimmed hat with a buckle in the front that you're used to seeing around Thanksgiving.)

Pilgrim sells chicken. Lots and lots of chicken. You've probably eaten some of Bo's chicken.

The Pilgrim's Pride company website (www.pilgrimspride.com, as you may have guessed) tells the story of how Pilgrim joined his brother in business after the brother and a partner bought a small feed store in 1946. Bo showed great initiative and continually improved the small business. Eventually, brother Bo led in the acquisition of other businesses. He became sole owner of the enterprise after his brother's untimely death.

Today, Pilgrim's Pride is the largest chicken company in the world, with well over 50,000 employees and over $7 billion in annual sales.

That's billion with a "B".

Now Bo is not eccentric in the way that some folks are eccentric. The face of the giant Bo Pilgrim head, for example, is decidedly dour. But he does have a fairly unique sense of humor. He has appeared in a number of television commercials clutching "Henrietta," a white chicken, and wearing his famous pilgrim hat, usually repeating his trademark phrase in his trademark Texas drawl, "I won't sell a fat, yella chicken."

Pilgrim also exhibited his flair for the eccentric (and, possibly, the illegal) when he strode into the Texas Senate and started handing out checks for $10,000 while legislators were preparing to vote on a controversial workers' compensation bill. Turns out, you can't do that. While Pilgrim did not receive any punishment for this action, the authors of *Weird Texas* note that he did learn "a valuable lesson...which he was able to sum up in three words: 'automatic fund transfer.'"

Chapter 13

"The Queen of Ice Cream"

Amy Miller Simmons
?-present

Name: Amy Miller Simmons
Lived: ?-present
Texas connection: Lives in Austin
Occupation: Ice cream baroness
Claim to weirdness: An application for a job at Amy's Ice Cream is a paper bag
Tex-centricity Scale: 6 scoops (out of 10)

You *have to* go to Amy's Ice Cream. And when you do, I recommend Mexican Vanilla with a Twix bar crushed in.

Here's what will happen. You will watch some zany person scoop ice cream out of a freezer and slap it down onto a countertop. He or she may very well throw the ice cream up into the air at some point—it's ice cream as performance art.

Then, after the ice cream is lying on the counter, the Scoop (that's what they call the people who serve ice cream at Amy's) will slap the mound of ice cream with the back of his or her spoon. It will make a loud sound and you will possibly jump. Then, after the ice cream is flat and round, like a creamy, cold pancake, the Scoop will take a Twix bar from a freezer and lay it on top of the ice cream. He or she will then fold the ice cream over the Twix bar like a tortilla and then proceed to butcher the concoction until the candy bar is thoroughly "crushed in," to borrow the Amy's lingo.

The whole show is quite enjoyable, as my seven-year-old son will tell you. And then comes the best part—eating it. The ice cream is incredibly rich and creamy, and you will definitely need a drink afterwards to wash the thick sweetness out of your mouth.

I might take a moment to recommend the large size in a sugar cone. You won't be able to finish it. But it'll be fun to try.

Amy Miller Simmons got her start in the ice cream business back when she was just Amy Miller, a student at Tufts University in Boston. She worked for a local ice cream establishment there and got her hands dirty in the business end of things by helping the owner to expand into other markets.

When Amy relocated to Austin, she brought her knowledge of ice cream with her. She also brought a conviction that she was selling an experience more than a dessert. She and a partner wrote a hot check to lease their first Austin property and sold shares in the nascent business to friends and former co-workers.

Since then, the business has grown steadily. As of this writing, there are 10 stores in Austin, two in San Antonio, and one in Houston. Potential applicants are not given a job application. Instead, they're given a white paper bag and told to "be creative." Amy's management encourages Scoops to do tricks with ice cream and even trains them periodically to learn new ones. While they offer a total of over 300 ice cream flavors, they only have seven at a time at any given location. They also offer dozens of toppings that can be crushed in to the ice cream. "Crush'ns" include Kit Kats, fresh strawberries, Oreos, Cameos, bananas, graham crackers, and many other goodies.

The ice cream chain's mission statement is simple: "Make people's day." Amy Miller Simmons says, "What we know is that people come into the ice cream store here not 'cause they're hungry. They're here 'cause they're with their family and they want to experience something together or some special moment."

Zaniness is a way of life at Amy's Ice Cream. From the funny cow décor to the antics of the help, a visit to Amy's is a visit to a shrine of Austin eccentricity. They even have a flavor of ice cream named after another eccentric Texan, Austin musician Roky Erickson. Celebrities including the late Governor Ann Richards, newsman Dan Rather and actress Sandra Bullock have passed through Amy's doors. And $3.5 million in annual sales have passed through her coffers, thanks to the experience (and the ice cream) that she offers her customers.

In the meantime, Amy Miller Simmons has been featured in several books on business and in magazines such as *Inc.* and *Texas Business Weekly*. In addition to making money and serving her customers, Amy has made a point of being active in service to her community. She has offered free ice cream to blood donors and schoolchildren, has participated actively in business affairs affecting other Austin restaurant owners, and has partnered with a variety of local charities to make an impact in the communities where her ice cream shops are located.

Amy Miller Simmons has captured the essence of eclectic Austin fun and rolled it all up into a franchise that is as profitable as it is silly.

Chapter 14
"Are We There, Yeti?"

Tom Slick
1916-1962

Name: Thomas Baker Slick, Jr.
Lived: 1916-1962
Texas connection: Lived in San Antonio
Occupation: Oilman, aviation entrepreneur, inventor, author, philanthropist
Claim to weirdness: Hunted Bigfoot and the Abominable Snowman
Tex-centricity Scale: 7 giant footprints (out of 10)

Tom Slick, Jr., inherited millions when his father Tom, Sr. (the "King of the Wildcatters"), died unexpectedly at age 46. This left Tom, Jr., in the enviable position of being a good-looking young multi-millionaire with a degree from Yale and famous friends like Howard Hughes and Jimmy Stewart.

He had looks, money, intelligence, and connections. Tom Slick could do anything he wanted with his life. So, what did he want to do?

Why, find the Abominable Snowman, of course!

But Tom Slick wasn't totally loony. He was sane enough to be highly successful in a variety of business endeavors. First, his father's thriving oil business became even more profitable under his leadership. Later, he and his brother founded Slick Airways, a successful cargo airline that eventually flew supplies to troops in Vietnam as part of Air America. He dipped his toes into the construction industry and ended up inventing the "lift slab" method of construction, still in use today. Slick also tried his hand—and found success—in the cattle, mining, real estate, and invention businesses. Respectively, he helped to develop the Brangus breed of beef cattle, restarted defunct diamond mines in Africa, owned mineral rights in several states and Mexico, and earned at least three patents for his inventions.

Tom Slick was also successful in establishing major research institutions, including the Mind Science Foundation, the Southwest Research Institute, the Southwest Foundation for Biomedical Research, the Institute of Inventive Research, the Southwest Agricultural Institute, and the Human Progress Foundation. The first three are still functioning today. According to a biography of Slick found at the Mind Science Foundation website (www.mindscience.org), the Southwest Research Institute alone has 2800 employees and revenues in the hundreds of millions of dollars. The Southwest Foundation for Biomedical Research, meanwhile, has hundreds of employees and was the site of the first baboon-to-human heart transplant.

Notwithstanding his other accomplishments, Tom Slick also found time to serve in the Navy, to serve on the War Production Board during World War II, to lounge at the Beverly Hills Hotel next door to Howard Hughes, and to write books about world peace, including Prentice-Hall's *Permanent Peace: A Check and Balance Plan*, published in 1958.

Tom Slick, like his friend Howard Hughes, proved that eccentricity need not preclude personal success.

Young Tom's taste for the marginally bizarre was whetted when he was still in college at Yale. In 1937 while traveling in Europe with friends, Tom took a side trip to Loch Ness, Scotland, to seek the famous water beast, Nessie. While there are no reports indicating that the group saw anything aside from water (and maybe some men in kilts), the trip apparently sparked a keen interest in Tom Slick. He would spend most of the 1950s searching for one cryptid after another all over the world: Yeti (the so-called "Abominable Snowman") in the Himalayas; Sasquatch (aka "Bigfoot") in the US Pacific Northwest; giant salamanders in California; lake monsters in Alaska; and Orang Pendek (a Bigfoot-like primate) in southeast Asia. Slick led some of these expeditions himself; others he organized or funded.

Slick did not plan to merely look for strange creatures. He planned to capture one alive and bring it back to San Antonio. On his popular cryptozoology website www.cryptomundo.com, Loren Coleman, author of the first published Tom Slick biography, writes, "Slick had built, on [the Southwest Foundation for Biomedical Research] site, a special area that was to house either a Yeti or a Bigfoot that he planned to have captured."

Tom's taste for adventure led him to personally head up his own expedition to the Himalayas in search of a Yeti. An interesting episode in the life of Tom Slick involves an artifact purported to be a Yeti hand that was kept as a relic in a monastery in Pangboche, Nepal. An associate of Slick's named Peter Byrne stole pieces of the hand, replaced them with human bones, and smuggled them out of Nepal in the luggage of actor Jimmy Stewart. They were examined by a primatologist with inconclusive results. Later, none other than

Sir Edmund Hillary examined the hand at the monastery—complete with the human bones Byrne had substituted—and found it to be a hoax.

The similarities between Tom Slick and his friend Howard Hughes are remarkable. Both hailed from Texas (though Tom was born in Pennsylvania); both made stacks of money in the aviation and oil industries; both were the sons of wealthy, flamboyant wildcatters; both were named after their fathers; both came into wealth at a young age and managed it expertly; both had shadowy ties to U.S. government activities; and both loved women—lots of women, by all accounts. In addition, both men survived airplane crashes. Hughes walked away from no fewer than four crashes; Slick made a forced landing in British Guiana after a diamond-hunting trip and spent two weeks living with a tribe of Waiwai.

Tom Slick's adventurous life came to an end before he ever found any of the mysterious creatures he sought so diligently. He was involved in another aircraft incident in 1962, but this one was fatal. Tom's Beechcraft Bonanza 35 exploded and crashed in Montana, and he passed away at 46, the same age his father had been when he died.

Side note: Nicolas Cage was set to play the part of Tom Slick in a 1990s movie called *Tom Slick, Monster Hunter.* The movie never became reality.

Chapter 15

"Silver Dollar Jim"

Jim West
1903-1957

Name: James Marion West, Jr.
Lived: 1903-1957
Texas connection: Lived in Houston
Occupation: Oilman, attorney, policeman wannabe
Claim to weirdness: Painted all his cars blue; wore a diamond-studded badge
Tex-centricity Scale: 10 silver dollars (out of 10)

James Marion West, Jr., was a Houston native that the website www.houstonhistory.com calls "an attorney, oil man, cattle rancher and eccentric." Like many of the other eccentrics in these pages, West inherited much of his wealth from his father, a cattle and lumber man. West, Sr., had moved the family to Houston from Mississippi when little Jim was two years old.

The elder James Marion West was an upstanding citizen in Houston, indeed in the entire state of Texas. The December 1952 issue of *The Cattleman* magazine featured an article about West, Sr., which described him as a "capitalist, lumber king, oil man, publisher, cowman..." and went on to say that he preferred the title of "cowman" over all the others because he was "a quiet, unassuming person despite his great wealth."

West, Sr., served as the 16th president of the Texas and Southwestern Cattle Raiser's Association, president of the Fort Terrett Ranch Company, president of the South Texas Hardwood Manufacturing Company, co-organizer of the South Texas Petroleum Company, a principal in the Gage Cattle Company, a director of numerous banks, a director on the boards of colleges and universities, manager of the West Lumber Company, publisher of the Dallas *Journal*, and stockholder in the Austin *Tribune*. He was appointed chairman of the Texas Highway Commission in 1939, but failed to earn Senate confirmation because he had supported a Republican presidential candidate in 1936. West, Sr., also established the West Foundation "for charitable, religious, educational, and scientific purposes."

James, Jr., was a little less quiet and unassuming than his father. He earned the nickname "Silver Dollar Jim" from his habit of tossing silver dollars to passersby on the street and to regularly tipping waiters, doormen, and valets with the coinage. According to a 2002 article in Houston's *The Scene* magazine, Jim West kept hundreds of silver dollars on hand for tips and also for "his own amusement." The article notes that the wealthy eccentric enjoyed throwing the coins on the floor at restaurants and watching the waitresses scramble for them. He also had a penchant for throwing silver dollars into his pool during parties and watching guests dive after them.

West was a fervent supporter of law enforcement, particularly the Houston Police Department. One biographer states that he was known for "chasing criminals right behind the police." Another website calls West, Jr., a "policeman wannabe." Jim West went on patrols with police officers, attended their conferences, and let the HPD have access to the massive receiver at a radio station he owned.

In the literary classic *The Big Book of Duh: A Bathroom Book*, author Bob Fenster relates that Jim West once joined the Texas Rangers and had a special badge commissioned, one that was studded with diamonds. "Don't you think suspects felt special getting arrested by a Ranger with a diamond badge?" Fenster asks.

Sources note that Jim West had somewhere between 30 and 40 cars, mostly Cadillacs, which he kept stocked with an arsenal of guns. Many of these cars bristled with antennas. At one time, West grew infatuated with the color blue and had every personal and business vehicle that he owned painted that color. Textbook Texas eccentricity.

The younger West died in 1957. The legendary Texas oilman and attorney was 54 years old. Very few characters in the history of Texas embody the spirit of Texas eccentricity quite the way that Jim West did. In the decidedly accurate words of the Great Houstonians website, James Marion West, Jr., "typified the spirit of the so-called 'eccentric Texas Millionaire' [sic] if anyone did."

Part 2
Peculiar Politicians

Eccentric Texas politicians have taken to the national stage on a couple of occasions in the past few decades. Most recently, it was Ron Paul, former Libertarian candidate for President who ran in the 2008 race as a long-shot Republican and who set single-day Internet fundraising records. Before Ron Paul came along, however, there was H. Ross Perot, a Dallas billionaire who ran for President twice and captivated the nation with his folksy speeches and ubiquitous charts and graphs. He received a larger share of the popular vote than any third-party candidate since Teddy Roosevelt and single-handedly did more to solidify the concept of the Texas eccentric in the national consciousness than anyone before or since.

But eccentrics existed in Texas politics long before they ever hit the national scene. In this section we'll take a look at the lives of men who became governor, men who became President, and men like Clayton Williams who never quite made it into office but nonetheless left a trail of political goofiness for the rest of us to enjoy.

Chapter 16

"The Law West of the Pecos"

Judge Roy Bean
c. 1825-1903

Name: Phantly Roy Bean
Lived: c. 1825-1903
Texas connection: Lived in the "Beanville" slum of San Antonio and in Pecos County
Occupation: Saloon-keeper and justice of the peace, at the same time
Claim to weirdness: Held court in his saloon and made jurors buy drinks during recess
Tex-centricity Scale: 10 gavels (out of 10)

This prototypical Texas eccentric has lent his name to a roller coaster, "The Judge Roy Scream" at Six Flags over Texas, and has lent his story to movies such as *The Westerner* starring Gary Cooper and *The Life and Times of Judge Roy*

Bean starring Paul Newman. There was even a short-lived television series named after him in the 1950s.

Compared to Phantly Roy Bean, other characters in these pages may seem positively dull. Few compare to him when it comes to outrageous behavior.

Bean was born into a poor family in Kentucky and left home at sixteen to follow his adventurous brothers all over the country. After getting into trouble in New Orleans, Bean jumped from San Antonio, Texas, to Chihuahua, Mexico, where he and a brother operated a trading post. After shooting and killing a local man, Bean fled first to Sonora, Mexico, and then to San Diego, where another Bean brother was soon to be elected mayor. After wounding a man there in a duel, Bean was jailed for two months before he escaped and fled. Along the way, he killed a Mexican officer in a duel over a woman and was almost lynched by the victim's friends. They strung him by the neck to a tree branch and left him sitting on top of his horse. The horse didn't bolt, though, and after the men left, the woman he had dueled over came and cut him down.

Bean settled temporarily in New Mexico and tended bar in another brother's saloon. During the Civil War, he joined a Texas Army unit leaving New Mexico and ended up in San Antonio. Over the next two decades, Bean would engage in a series of shady business undertakings and live with his wife and five kids in a slum that came to be called "Beanville." Some of Bean's businesses included selling firewood he had cut from a neighbor's land, selling milk he thinned with creek water, and selling meat he obtained from rustling unbranded cattle in the area. He ended up operating a saloon in Beanville.

Bean's political career started after he left San Antonio and settled among railroad workers encamped in West Texas. He set up a small saloon among the burgeoning population of laborers and soon was pressed into service by Texas Rangers desperate for some sort of judicial presence in the area. He was named Justice of the Peace of a new precinct in 1882 and promptly labeled himself "The Law West of the Pecos." He famously held court in his saloon. Historian Joe Tom Davis notes that "Bean relied on a single lawbook, the 1879 edition of the *Revised Statutes of Texas*. If newer lawbooks appeared, Bean used them as kindling."

Bean enjoyed a reputation as a hard judge, although his toughness was probably exaggerated. One account contends that he never sentenced anyone to jail and only sentenced two men to hang, and one of those escaped. Another historian holds that Bean never sent anyone to the penitentiary but sentenced several men to hang, then invariably arranged for his staff to make it possible for them to escape prior to the date of the hanging.

"The Jersey Lilly" from the National Archives

Bean moved his saloon and courtroom as the railroad progressed westward. He named his new saloon the Jersey Lilly, supposedly in honor of actress Lilly Langtry. The settlement where it was located came to be known as Langtry.

One of the more eccentric rulings under Judge Roy Bean included a finding in the case of an Irishman who had killed a Chinese railroad worker that homicide was the killing of a human being, but that the lawbook didn't say anything about killing a Chinaman. (It just so happened that there was a mob of angry Irishmen outside his courtroom when he made that particular judgment.) In another famous case, the judge fined a dead man the exact contents of his pockets, which he then used to buy the man a casket and a burial plot.

Bean was characteristically averse to following rules. He refused to send the state its portion of fines he received in his court, and he granted divorces, something he wasn't technically allowed to do. After he was voted out of office in 1896, he refused to give up his gavel and continued to hear cases.

Bean is often confused with an eccentric judge from Arkansas, "Hanging" Isaac Parker. In reality, Bean was apparently more kind and generous than he ever let on in his courtroom. He gave a great deal of the money he took in from fines to the poor. His generous ways continued even after he no longer held office. According to John Troesser, writing for www.TexasEscapes.com, "Bean enjoyed his tough reputation and he kept his kindness hidden. Throughout the years, he took some of the fines and much of the collected goods and gave them to the poor and destitute of the area, doing so without it being known. He even took monies collected in the Jersey Lilly, his own trackside saloon, and used them to buy medicine for the sick and poor in and around Langtry."

In 1896, Bean became something of a national celebrity after hosting a world championship boxing match on a sandbar in the Rio Grande. The organizers of the bout hadn't been able to locate a venue in the U.S. due to rules against boxing in several states, including Texas. Reporters and fight fans descended on the Jersey Lilly in the remote Texas desert and then crossed a crude bridge onto the "island" and watched Bob Fitzsimmons knock out Peter Maher in 95 seconds. When sportswriters wired their stories all over the country, Roy Bean became a nationally-known character.

Bean died after a night of heavy drinking. It's reported that

71

he was depressed over the changing times, as a power plant was on the verge of bringing electricity to his distant corner of the Lone Star State. He will undoubtedly be remembered forever as one of the most eccentric of Texas' historical figures.

Chapter 17

"The Man with the Knife"

Jim Bowie
c. 1825-1903

Name: James Bowie
Lived: 1796-1836
Texas connection: Died at the Alamo
Occupation: Land speculator and hero
Claim to weirdness: That ever-present knife and those sideburns
Tex-centricity Scale: 2 Bowie knives (out of 10)

Like fellow Texas crazy person Roy Bean, Jim Bowie was a Kentuckian by birth and a Texan by choice. He grew up on the frontier in Kentucky, Georgia, and Louisiana, learning English, Spanish, and French, and he developed toughness and an aptitude with rifles, pistols, and knives. Before moving to Texas, Bowie made a living in Louisiana by speculating in land

and slaves, and he made a name for himself by surviving an attack in which he was stabbed multiple times and shot at least twice, by several men. The end of that famous fight, dubbed the "Sandbar Fight," resulted in Bowie's adversary, Sheriff Norris Wright, dying at the blade of Bowie's huge hunting knife. The killing of Wright was quickly attributed to self-defense, even by Wright's supporters, and it was widely accepted that Bowie hadn't started the fight and only drew out his knife after someone had shot at him.

News of Bowie's courage and of his giant, deadly knife spread quickly, reaching as far away as England, and Bowie's style of knife became popular worldwide. Bowie's brother Rezin explained that he had made that particular knife for his brother for hunting and that Jim Bowie only started carrying it for protection after he had been shot at by an adversary prior to the Sandbar Fight, possibly Wright. He also contended that his brother only used it in the Sandbar affair to save his life after he had been shot.

In William Kennedy's *Texas: The Rise, Progress, and Prospects of the Republic of Texas*, published in 1841, Rezin Bowie is quoted as having said that, "...the knife was used only as a defensive weapon, and not till he had been shot down; it was the means of saving his life....I would here assert also, that neither Colonel James Bowie nor myself, at any period of our lives, ever had a duel with any person whatsoever."

While tales of Bowie's bravery and honorableness in a fight were recounted far and wide, stories of some of his business exploits were less advertised. Bowie and his family had run into legal problems in Louisiana for selling land that they never owned, apparently using forged deeds. Bowie and his brother also became involved in the slave trade at one point, buying slaves from the pirate Jean Lafitte and selling them in Louisiana.

After the Sandbar Fight, Bowie moved to Texas, converted

to Roman Catholicism and became a Mexican citizen. He took up residence in San Antonio and began buying Lone Star land. A little over a year after he settled permanently in Texas, in 1831, he married the 19-year-old daughter of his business partner, the former *alcalde* of San Antonio, who was later to become Mexico's vice governor of the province.

In the years after he married, James Bowie traveled much—as a married man, I fully understand this urge. In an event that was later "recorded as a remarkable instance of courage, physical endurance, and presence of mind," Bowie and eight others set out "for the silver mines of the San Saba River, and were followed by 164 Towackanie and Caddo Indians." A battle ensued wherein Bowie and his companions were attacked by the much larger native force. Meanwhile, a group of Comanches arrived in San Antonio and reported to the people there that Bowie's party was going to be attacked by a force many times larger than their own. The people, including Bowie's wife, began to mourn, assuming the men would never survive. They were surprised when Bowie and his men returned very much alive, save for one man, who was very much dead. The Indians, it was reported, lost dozens of men during their thirteen-hour attack on Bowie's party.

Despite his heroics, Bowie was reportedly a schemer who, while heavily in debt, portrayed himself as a man of wealth. Attached to the prominent Veramendí family, he had access to funds from his wife's family. Nonetheless, Bowie spent little time at home with his wife, choosing instead to chase adventure by seeking lost silver mines and serving as colonel of the volunteer militia.

In 1833, Bowie made his first foray into armed conflict between Anglo colonists and the Mexican military. He inserted himself into a clash between a Mexican military officer named Piedras and the citizens of Nacogdoches. Piedras had commanded the citizens to disarm. The citizens refused, a fight resulted, and Bowie raced to the scene of the antagonism.

Having lost 33 men in the conflict with the townspeople, Piedras left the town, and Bowie led 18 men to ambush his force. As the ambush played out, Piedras fled, and Bowie marched the captured Mexican soldiers back to Nacogdoches, victorious.

After establishing his reputation as a man of skill and more than a little luck in matters of armed conflict in the Sandbar Fight, the Caddo ambush, and the Battle of Nacogdoches, Bowie went on to earn distinction in other fights. In 1835, he found himself encamped with the leaders of the Texas Revolution—Stephen F. Austin, William Travis, and James Fannin, among others—and was instructed to take 92 men on a scouting mission. During the course of this mission, Bowie and his men were attacked by a Mexican force of 300 cavalry and 100 infantry. In the hours-long battle that followed, Bowie captured the Mexicans' cannon and only lost one man. Sixteen Mexicans were killed, with still more wounded. Years later, a Texian in the fight named Noah Smithwick wrote, "Bowie was a born leader, never needlessly spending a bullet or imperiling a life. His voice is still ringing in my old deaf ears as he repeatedly admonished us, 'Keep under cover boys and reserve your fire. We haven't a man to spare.'" Bowie and company's battle for the Mexican cannon is known today as the Battle of Concepción.

The next fight for Bowie has come to be known as the Grass Fight. In it, he led a group of thirty horsemen against a train carrying supplies to the Mexican forces in San Antonio. In the ensuing confrontation, the Mexicans lost 60 men. The train, rumored among the Texians to be full of silver, turned out instead to be full of fresh grass for the Mexicans' garrisoned horses, much to the disappointment of Bowie's men.

Bowie's next military adventure would not turn out so well. He arrived with thirty men at the Alamo in San Antonio on January 19, 1836, and found 78 soldiers inside, all of them demoralized and poorly clothed. William Travis, along with thirty more men, arrived soon after, and David Crockett rode in with twelve Tennessee volunteers a few days later. Bowie was elected commander of the forces inside the Alamo but ended up sharing command with Travis, a commissioned officer. As thousands of Mexican troops advanced on San Antonio, Bowie wrote letters to other leaders of the Texas revolution asking for men, money, and munitions.

At some point during his time inside the Alamo, Bowie fell seriously ill. He remained bedridden until the end. When William Travis famously drew a line in the sand at the Alamo and asked that any man willing to stay and fight cross over it, Bowie, according to some reports, insisted that his cot be carried across.

On March 6, the Mexicans attacked and all those inside the Alamo died. Reports of Bowie's manner of death range from him being brought out alive on his bed and having his tongue cut out by a Mexican commander, to him being thrown alive onto the funeral pyre, to him shooting himself. The generally accepted story is that he died in his bed, defending himself with pistols and his famous knife.

A short-lived television series about Bowie, called "The Adventures of Jim Bowie," aired in the 1950s.

James Bowie, land speculator, gambler, soldier, slave trader, and adventurer, left behind him a trail of exploits that have earned him a heralded status in Texas history as one of the most colorful and bravest characters the state has ever known.

Chapter 18

"King of the Wild Frontier"

Davy Crockett
c. 1825-1903

Name: David Crockett
Lived: 1786-1836
Texas connection: Died at the Alamo
Occupation: U.S. Representative, frontiersman and soldier
Claim to weirdness: He named his rifles Betsy, Old Betsy, and Pretty Betsy
Tex-centricity Scale: 2 coonskin hats (out of 10)

David Crockett's story begins with him leaving home at an early age to avoid a whipping at the hands of his father for skipping school. He spent years wandering around Tennessee and learned how to survive as a hunter and trapper during this youthful odyssey.

Returning home at 19 years of age, Crockett soon married

and started a family. In 1813 he enlisted in the Tennessee volunteers and fought in the Creek War under Andrew Jackson. In 1826, after serving in several local posts and also in the Tennessee legislature, Crockett was elected to the U.S. House of Representatives. He became something of a celebrity along the way, as tales of his exploits and his frontier childhood had reached the East via a book about him written by another man, a man who didn't attach his own name to the book in hopes that readers would think it written by Davy Crockett himself. Crockett soon wrote his own book in response and toured the East to promote it.

Crockett would be re-elected twice more, and when he lost a bid for re-election in 1835, he reportedly said, "You may all go to hell, and I will go to Texas."

Crockett proceeded to Texas and found it a veritable paradise. He saw opportunities to make a fortune in land and possibly to restore his political career. In a letter dated January 9, 1836, he wrote, "I must say as to what I have seen of Texas it is the garden spot of the world. The best land and the best prospects for health I ever saw, and I do believe it is a fortune to any man to come here. There is a world of country here to settle...I am rejoiced at my fate. I had rather be in my present situation than to be elected to a seat in Congress for life. I am in hopes of making a fortune yet for myself and family, bad as my prospect has been."

Crockett did not immediately intend to join the war for Texas independence, but he was drawn into the fight. He joined the defenders of the Alamo and, on March 6, 1836, died at the hands of a Mexican force led by General Antonio López de Santa Anna.

Some controversy surrounds Crockett's death. A single diary holds that he was taken as a prisoner to Santa Anna and executed, but the eyewitness accounts of the only American survivors of the Alamo—William Travis' slave Joe and an elderly woman named Susanna Dickinson—hold that they saw

Crockett dead "between the long barracks and the chapel," and "with the bodies of slain Mexican soldiers around him."

Crockett's legend has survived and even grown since his death. A number of movies, plays, and television series about him have been produced. Davy Crockett crazes hit the U.S., the UK, and, bizarrely, Egypt—with coonskin caps a hot seller among kids. "The Ballad of Davy Crockett" hit number one on the *Billboard* music charts in 1955. (Interestingly, four different versions of the song hit the charts that year, and three of them were once in the Top 10 simultaneously.) Historians contend, however, that David Crockett never went by the name Davy in his lifetime.

Crockett's impact on the histories of two different states is undeniable, as is his legendary status as a frontiersman, soldier, story-teller, and adventurer.

Chapter 19

"Last of the Jewish Cowboys"

Kinky Friedman
1944-present

Name: Richard S. Friedman
Lived: 1944-present
Texas connection: Raised in Central Texas; lives near Austin
Occupation: Singer-songwriter, author, columnist, gubernatorial candidate
Claim to weirdness: Motto for his run at the governorship was "Why the hell not?"
Tex-centricity Scale: 7 cigars (out of 10)

Kinky Friedman is nothing if not eccentric. Known for cigars, irreverence, and cowboy shtick, Friedman has made his living raising eyebrows, starting with his early days in the music business.

Friedman's first band released an album that parodied the

surf music that was popular at the time. His second band, Kinky Friedman and the Texas Jewboys, released a series of satirical country and western songs and managed to get signed by a major label. He toured with Bob Dylan twice in the 1970s.

When his music career slowed in the 1980s, Friedman began writing detective novels. His books feature a fictionalized version of himself, along with fictionalized versions of friends and acquaintances, solving crimes. Like his music, Friedman's fiction is irreverent. To date, Friedman has published 26 books. From 2001-2004 he wrote a regular column for *Texas Monthly*.

In 2003, Friedman mocked the nude appearance of the Dixie Chicks in *Entertainment Weekly* by appearing naked in three different poses on the cover of the *Dallas Observer*.

Friedman ran for the governorship of Texas in 2004 as an Independent, leading a colorful campaign with slogans like, "He ain't Kinky, he's my governor," "My governor is a Jewish cowboy," "Why the hell not?" and "How hard could it be?" He received several hundred thousand dollars in donations from his friend, hair products multi-millionaire John McCall, and received support from people like Willie Nelson, Don Imus, and Jimmy Buffett. His campaign was known for Friedman's zany quips and political incorrectness. Friedman won just over 11 percent of the vote, which was good enough for fourth place in the five-person race. He has held out the possibility of running again in 2010, this time as a Democrat. He argues that God couldn't win the governorship if he ran as an Independent.

Few characters in the history of Texas politics have been as deliberately controversial and as rabidly tactless as Friedman. His public persona as a cigar-chomping, whiskey-swilling lecher has done little to diminish his cult popularity as a public figure in Texas. He writes novels and magazine articles that are widely read and has appeared frequently on television shows both regionally and nationally. And the legend of Kinky doesn't appear set to fade anytime soon.

Chapter 20

"LBJ"

Lyndon Baines Johnson
1908-1973

Name: Lyndon Baines Johnson
Lived: 1908-1973
Texas connection: Born in Stonewall, Texas
Occupation: President of the United States from 1963 to 1969
Claim to weirdness: "The Treatment" and his Amphicar
Tex-centricity Scale: 6 draft tickets (out of 10)

Known to most simply as "LBJ," Lyndon B. Johnson was the 36th President of the United States. He took office following the assassination of John F. Kennedy. He was known for passing the Civil Rights Act, creating Medicare and Medicaid, jump-starting America's space program, and dramatically escalating the United States' involvement in the Vietnam Conflict.

Johnson was born into a farming family and was, for a time, a high school teacher in Houston. He moved into politics by working as a secretary for a Texas Congressman. During his time as a political aide, Johnson met Claudia Alta Taylor (known to all as Lady Bird), the daughter of a wealthy East Texas cotton farmer. Johnson proposed marriage on their first date; she accepted his proposal 10 weeks later.

Lyndon and Lady Bird were married in 1934. Not long after, Lady Bird financed Johnson's first foray into politics with $10,000 from her sizable inheritance. In 1937, Johnson won a congressional seat for the first time. He would win re-election many times after that.

In 1960, Johnson entered the Presidential race. When it became evident that he was going to lose the nomination to John F. Kennedy, the Texan accepted an offer to be Kennedy's running mate. John F. Kennedy was assassinated in Dallas in 1963, and Johnson became the second Texas-born President (after Dwight D. Eisenhower). He was sworn into office aboard Air Force One by Sarah T. Hughes, a female federal judge who was a friend of his family. This made LBJ the only President ever to be sworn in by a female.

LBJ being sworn in aboard Air Force One

Johnson ran for re-election in 1964 and won easily over conservative darling Barry Goldwater. During his second term,

Johnson's popularity waned. Race riots, discontent over the Vietnam conflict, and high taxes that supported Johnson's social programs all contributed to his loss of support among the populace, as did an emerging distrust of his leadership.

Johnson had used two supposed attacks on U.S. warships in the Gulf of Tonkin as a pretext for seeking an expanded US role in Vietnam. Much later Johnson admitted that the second of the two attacks never happened. Despite the expanded role Congress granted him, Johnson's approach to the war was one of containment. In other words, the U.S. would neither win nor lose the war, only contain the North Vietnamese. Neither doves, who wanted the U.S. out of Vietnam altogether, nor hawks, who would be satisfied with nothing short of absolute victory, supported Johnson's approach.

On March 31, 1968, Johnson shocked the country by announcing that he would not seek re-election. He died of a heart attack a mere five years later at his ranch in Johnson City.

Johnson's legacy lives on in Texas. He has a city, a lake, a major freeway, and a space center named after him. He is remembered as a larger-than-life Texan, but also a larger-than-life eccentric.

Chief among Johnson's quirks was something that came to be called "The Treatment" in Washington, D.C. In *Lyndon B. Johnson: The Exercise of Power*, Rowland Evans and Robert Novak describe "The Treatment" this way:

> The Treatment could last ten minutes or four hours. It came, enveloping its target, at the LBJ Ranch swimming pool, in one of LBJ's offices, in the Senate cloakroom, on the floor of the Senate itself — wherever Johnson might find a fellow Senator within his reach.
>
> Its tone could be supplication, accusation, cajolery, exuberance, scorn, tears, complaint and the hint of threat. It was all of these together. It ran the gamut of human emotions. Its velocity was breathtaking, and it

was all in one direction. Interjections from the target were rare. Johnson anticipated them before they could be spoken. He moved in close, his face a scant millimeter from his target, his eyes widening and narrowing, his eyebrows rising and falling. From his pockets poured clippings, memos, statistics. Mimicry, humor, and the genius of analogy made The Treatment an almost hypnotic experience and rendered the target stunned and helpless.

Another odd trait for which Johnson became known was his legendary stinginess. He was a multimillionaire thanks to Lady Bird's investment of her inheritance in a struggling Austin television station, a move LBJ opposed. Despite his wealth, however, he insisted on turning lights off in rooms of the White House that were unoccupied, and he was known to wash and reuse Styrofoam cups.

Another Johnson idiosyncrasy was his fondness for a certain practical joke involving a rare vehicle called the Amphicar. Johnson regularly took dignitaries on tours of his Texas ranch in the Amphicar and, as he crested a hill beside his lake, the President would announce that the brakes had failed and proceed to drive right into the lake. Terrified passengers occasionally leapt from the car only to discover that the vehicle they had been riding in was amphibious. Johnson would then guide the Amphicar placidly across the water and they would all presumably share a laugh.

Oh, yeah—then there's this: Johnson regularly invited staffers into the restroom with him so that discussions wouldn't be interrupted by nature's inevitable call. This included, on one occasion, the female publisher of the *Washington Post.*

Couth was not an adjective that was used often in describing LBJ. In private conversation, it has been noted that Johnson frequently used colorful language, a fact that is clearly revealed in tapes released after he left office. One of the more famous quotes often attributed to LBJ is, "I never trust a man unless I've got his pecker in my pocket."

Here's hoping he rarely trusted other men.

In the end, Lyndon Baines Johnson, despite his unique foibles, passed more major legislation during his time in office than most Presidents, and his "Great Society" initiative was responsible for many of the social programs that are still in existence today. His life is a study in ambition, power, and, perhaps most important of all, Texas eccentricity.

Chapter 21

"Wild and Woolly"

Anthony Banning Norton
1821-1893

Name: Anthony Banning Norton
Lived: 1821-1893
Texas connection: Lived in Dallas and Henderson and Kaufman counties
Occupation: State legislator, military officer, newspaper editor, and local politician
Claim to weirdness: Vowed not to shave until Henry Clay was elected President
Tex-centricity Scale: 8 razors (out of 10)

In 1844, a committed Ohio Whig named Anthony Banning Norton publicly vowed not to shave his beard or trim his hair until Henry Clay was elected President of the United States. Alas, this never happened. And Norton kept his word.

Norton moved to Texas in 1848 and quickly became a state legislator. An adamant supporter of Sam Houston and a committed Unionist, Norton became an adjutant general in Houston's government. He also became editor of a Unionist newspaper in Austin.

After the outbreak of the Civil War, Norton was forced to move to the North. At the end of the hostilities, he returned to Texas and ran for governor, though he didn't win election. He moved to Dallas later and lived out his life there, filling a variety of local political positions, publishing newsletters and writing books. Norton was remembered after his death as "A Pioneer Newspaper Man of the State."

His untrimmed locks and whiskers left him with another reputation as well: that of inveterate eccentric. In fact, in his book about odd characters in Texas history, Gene Fowler assigned the title "Full-blown Eccentric" to the chapter about Anthony Banning Norton. In an article entitled "When You and I Were Young," Fanny Segur Foster remembers Norton this way, "When we came to Dallas in 1890, he was frequently seen on the streets, and his long, white beard, and his long, white hair bore witness to his youthful vow never to shave or have his hair cut if Henry Clay was not elected president."

There is little doubt that the flowing white locks made Norton easily recognizable in his time, and he remains one of the most unique Texas characters of the 19th century.

Chapter 22

"Pass the Biscuits, Pappy"

"Pappy" O'Daniel
1890-1969

Name: Wilbert Lee O'Daniel
Lived: 1890-1969
Texas connection: Lived in Fort Worth and Austin
Occupation: Governor of Texas from 1939-1941
Claim to weirdness: Pitched Hillbilly Flour and the 10 Commandments in campaign speeches
Tex-centricity Scale: 9 biscuits (out of 10)

Pappy O'Daniel was one of the most colorful but least effective governors in the history of Texas. He wasn't originally a politician; he was a flour mill sales manager. And it showed after he took office.

O'Daniel moved to Fort Worth to work for Burrus Mills in 1925. After taking over the mill's radio advertising, he began proclaiming the benefits of the flour and giving religious messages on the air. His zany radio announcements soon developed a following. He started writing songs and hired a band called the Light Crust Doughboys, which included a little-known fiddler named Bob Wills. O'Daniel eventually dismissed the band because he didn't like their "hillbilly music," but a public outcry forced him to bring them back. As part of the deal that brought about their return, the musicians had to agree to work in his mill in addition to playing on the radio show. The band was a hit, and the show was soon carried on radio stations throughout Texas and Oklahoma.

In 1935, O'Daniel formed his own flour company, Hillbilly Flour, after being fired from Burrus Mills. He continued his endeavors as a popular radio personality and formed a new band, The Hillbilly Boys. He was encouraged by his listeners to run for governor in 1938. A natural public speaker, he "stressed the Ten Commandments, the virtues of his own Hillbilly Flour, and the need for old-age pensions, tax cuts, and industrialization." He appealed to the rural populace and easily defeated other candidates in debates. He won the Democratic nomination which, at that time in Texas, meant he had won the election.

His two terms as governor were marked by a flurry of proposals that were voted down by legislators and by a series of broken campaign promises. He followed his time as governor by seeking (and obtaining) election as a U.S. Senator. His time in the Senate was characterized by anti-communist and anti-union rhetoric—he continued delivering fiery radio broadcasts, often lambasting the popular President Franklin Roosevelt.

O'Daniel chose not to seek re-election after opinion polls showed that he only had seven percent support.

After leaving politics, O'Daniel settled in the Dallas-Fort Worth metroplex and invested in land and an insurance company. He attempted a few unsuccessful political comebacks and "ranted about blood running in the streets because of the 'Communist-inspired' Supreme Court decision desegregating the nation's schools."

Pappy O'Daniel inspired a character by the same name in the Coen Brothers' 2000 film *O Brother, Where Art Thou?*

His inimitable personality made him a radio personality, candidate, and governor like no other, and a true Texas eccentric, if ever there was one.

Chapter 23

"The Ringtail Panther"

Martin Parmer
1778-1850

Name: Martin Parmer
Lived: 1778-1850
Texas connection: Died in Jasper County, Texas
Occupation: Missouri state legislator; Texas soldier, judge, and politician
Claim to weirdness: Called himself a "ringtail panther," apparently with a straight face
Tex-centricity Scale: 9 fistfights (out of 10)

Martin Parmer (his original surname was Palmer, but he changed it after he got into some legal trouble) moved from Virginia to Kentucky to Tennessee to Missouri to Arkansas to Texas. While in Missouri, he served on the state assembly, served in the state senate, and fought Indians as a state militia officer.

Parmer displayed his eccentricity early on. In the introduction to his book *Mavericks: A Gallery of Texas Characters*, Gene Fowler notes the following:

> Before heading for Texas in 1825, Parmer served in the Missouri legislature, where he informed fellow statesmen that he was "a Ring Tailed Painter [Panther] from Fishin' Creek, wild and woolly, hard to curry. When I'm mad, I fight, and when I fight, I *whip*. I raise my children to fight. I feed 'em on painters' [panthers'] hearts fried in rattlesnake grease."

After arriving in Texas, Parmer was a leader in the Fredonian Rebellion, "an unsuccessful attempt to liberate Texas from Mexico almost ten years before the Texas Revolution." Never afraid of a fight, Parmer also participated in the Battle of Gonzalez; and, prior to coming to Texas, had fought in the War of 1812. Later he became one of the men to sign the Texas Declaration of Independence.

Parmer married four times and had at least 16 children, not counting the six children one of his wives had from a previous marriage.

His historical significance is little doubted. A letter from a "Martin Palmer" dated March 6, 1836, and published in the New Orleans *True American* informed readers that committees in Texas were busily preparing a constitution and noted that "Travis' last express states San Antonio was strongly besieged; it is much feared that Travis and company are all massacred, as despatches [sic] have been due from that place three days and none have arrived here yet." This letter demonstrates the level of involvement of Parmer in the Texas Revolution. Minutes from several committee meetings also confirm that he was an important part of Texas history. Parmer County is named after him.

Historian Inez Smith Davis refers to the *History of Clay County* by W. H. Woodson to relate this story about the "Ring-Tailed Panther":

There was in those early days a Missourian who has been the hero of more than one singular story. This man was Martin Parmer, who because he so designated himself in moments of extreme gaiety was generally called the "Ring-tailed Painter." This man at one time was sent to Jefferson City as state senator. Like most Missourians he loved a fight, and being on the street one day when Governor Hugh McNair was about to interfere to settle a fight, the "Ring-tailed Painter," although a perfect stranger, promptly collared the Governor and backed him out of the circle. "A governor is no more in a fight than any other man," he later explained, "and he was like to spoil the prettiest kind of a fight."

That Parmer was a fighter there is little doubt. One historian notes that he was furthermore "a rough, uncouth, illiterate man, but of strong common sense and perfect integrity." The author of *The History of Caldwell and Livingston Counties, Missouri*, published in 1886, had this to say about Parmer:

Of this odd but somewhat noted character, Gen. W. Y. Slack thus writes, in an unfinished and unpublished manuscript sketch, now in existence, and which was written in about 1850: -

His habits and manners were as rude as his cabin, and like all other early pioneers, he was a true disciple of Esau, and lived by hunting. There were, however, but three kinds of game that "Ring Tail" Parmer cared

95

to expend ammunition upon, and these, as he expressed it, were "deers, bar and Injuns." The last named were not, in his judgment, the least worthy of his deadly aim. His warfare with the red men was not manly and open, but on the contrary was stealthy and murderous. [From what the compiler has learned from other sources the last sentence, regarding the style of Parmer's warfare against the Indians, is strictly correct.]

The traveler who called at Parmer's cabin and claimed his hospitality was furnished with dry deerskins for his bed, wild venison and wild honey for his repast. The ceiling of his cabin was lined with dried venison; one corner of the room was filled with green hams, another was occupied with a number of deer skins sewed up tight into sacks and filled with honey-comb, and another contained a pole scaffold fitted up as a bedstead. On two hooks over the rude fireplace hung his rifle, the most esteemed article of furniture about the household. Thus fitted up in life, and with such paraphernalia started the first settler in this great valley; and when the reader is introduced to Parmer's cabin and made acquainted with its arrangements and fixtures, he has been introduced to the domicile and its appointments of every early pioneer that first felled the forests and plowed the virgin soil of the Great West. Parmer's cabin, on Parmer's creek, formed the nucleus of a settlement which, in the course of a dozen years, extended along the hilly bluff lands as far northwest as Salt creek, and as far north (about eight miles) as the "great prairie" to which then even the hunters knew no limit.

Martin "Ring Tail" Parmer is one of the most remarkable characters in the annals of Texas, a larger-than-life frontiersman who was among a handful of people who led the way toward Texas' independence. Despite his eccentric persona, or perhaps because of it, he found himself in the midst of a tumultuous time in Texas and helped establish the peaceful future of the Republic.

Chapter 24

"Dr. No"

Ron Paul
1935-present

Name: Ronald Ernest Paul
Lived: 1935-present
Texas connection: Lives in East Texas
Occupation: US Representative and ob/gyn
Claim to weirdness: Refuses to accept his Congressional pension
Tex-centricity Scale: 4 FAFSAs (out of 10)

Ron Paul doesn't mind being different from those around him. His website quotes a former treasury secretary as saying that Paul is the "one exception to the Gang of 535" on Capitol Hill. Others relate the story of how John McCain once told Paul's campaign chair, "You're working for the most honest man in Congress." Sometimes being different is good.

Like many other Texas eccentrics, Paul wasn't born in Texas. He was born, instead, in Pennsylvania. Paul grew up poor and put himself through college with money he saved from odd jobs. He went on to medical school and became an ob/gyn.

After Paul was drafted, he served as a flight surgeon in military installations around the world during the Vietnam Conflict, though he was never sent to Vietnam itself. Near the end of his military career, he was stationed in San Antonio. While there, he first became involved in politics, assisting with Barry Goldwater's campaign for President.

After moving to the Lake Jackson area, Ron Paul began delivering babies—lots of babies, as he was the only baby doctor in the county for some time. He refused to accept Medicare or Medicaid out of principle—instead, he either delivered babies for free or arranged payment plans for parents who couldn't afford to pay up front.

Paul won his first congressional seat in 1976. He was re-elected many times during the 1980s. In 1988, he was the Libertarian Party's candidate for President, and he returned to Congress as a Republican in 1996. Paul was urged by supporters to enter the 2004 Presidential race, but chose not to. The same thing happened in the lead-up to the 2008 contest; this time, Paul dove in.

During his time in Congress, Paul has written and sponsored many bills, most aimed at limiting the size and scope of government. He is in favor of abolishing most federal bureaucracies, the federal income tax, and the Federal Reserve Bank. He prefers currency with gold backing, and he feels that states, not the federal government, should address social issues such as abortion, gay marriage, and governmental display of religious symbols like the Ten Commandments.

Paul claims to have voted against 700 bills that would have expanded government, and he has earned the nickname "Dr. No" in the halls of Congress. He even once voted against a bill that he had sponsored himself. Paul is a strict constitutionalist and feels that military conflicts should only be entered into when Congress formally declares war. He was one of only six Republicans to vote against the Iraq War Resolution, and he was the only Republican candidate for President in the 2008 campaign to have so voted.

Paul is one of the most unique legislators to have ever served in Washington, D.C., clearly driven by principle and sincerely concerned for his country. He believes that the income tax could be eliminated if wasteful government spending was stopped, and he has promised never to vote to raise taxes. That makes him eccentric in Washington if nowhere else.

Ron Paul has not only voted against virtually all new spending while in office, he has also, on a more personal level, refused to accept benefits funded with taxpayer money. He has repeatedly turned down the pension benefits to which he is entitled as a Congressman, and he refused to allow his children to fill out FAFSAs for federal student aid during their university studies—he didn't want his family contributing to government spending.

Though he was born in Pennsylvania, there can be little doubt that Ron Paul has become a seminal Texas maverick. There is no one in Washington quite like him.

Chapter 25

"The Giant Sucking Sound"

H. Ross Perot
1930-present

Name: Henry Ross Perot
Lived: 1930-present
Texas connection: Born in Texarkana
Occupation: Businessman
Claim to weirdness: Folksy sayings and charts and graphs
Tex-centricity Scale: 6 infomercials (out of 10)

Dallas businessman H. Ross Perot first came to national prominence in the late 1970s when two of his employees were imprisoned in Iran and he hired retired Special Forces Colonel Bull Simons to rescue them. The successful mission was followed by a best-selling book and a mini-series. Prior to this mission, Perot had done much to assist the US government behind the scenes. He specialized in efforts to get POWs out of

Southeast Asia, at one time even sending two airliners full of supplies to improve conditions for those held in prison camps. Though the air shipments were refused by the Vietnamese government, Perot's actions threw an international spotlight onto the fate of these American servicemen and may have improved their lot.

In Texas, Perot—by this time a billionaire as founder of Electronic Data Systems—got his start in politics by assisting then-governor Mark White in reforming education. Perot's committee came up with several new laws, all of which were eventually passed, including "No Pass, No Play," a controversial law that prevented students who had failed a class from participating in interscholastic sports and other competitions.

In time, Perot became a fierce critic of U.S. government policies, particularly those of President George H. W. Bush, and particularly in the aftermath of Project Desert Storm. In 1992, he told supporters that he would run for office as an Independent if they could get his name on the ballot in all 50 states. They did, and, though he subsequently dropped out of the race temporarily, he ultimately followed through with the Presidential run.

Perot, with his down-home accent and his country-fried sayings, quickly became a media darling. He was a guest on many news shows, was featured on the cover of *Time* magazine, and after he decided to officially enter the race, began investing millions of his own dollars in campaign advertising. Perot chose a novel means of promoting his candidacy—he purchased 30-minute blocks of premium television airtime and gave infomercials, rather than just the typical 30-second political ad.

Perot was invited to participate in three Presidential debates and performed well. In the debates as well as in his infomercials, he was noted for his use of data (often illustrated with charts and graphs), for his quick wit, and for his biting criticism of the way things were done in Washington, D. C. At one point, Perot led the candidates of both major parties—George H. W. Bush and Bill Clinton—in national polling.

In the end, Perot won 18.9 percent of the national vote in the election, the best showing for any third party candidate since Theodore Roosevelt. He qualified for government-matching funds in the 1996 election. Perot and his supporters started the Reform Party between the two elections, and Perot was again a frequent guest on television news programs. It was during this time that he coined the phrase "the giant sucking sound" in reference to the number of U.S. jobs being pulled across the Mexican border because of the North American Free Trade Agreement.

In the end, Perot fared worse in 1996—he had spent less of his own money on this campaign and hadn't been invited to participate in televised debates. In the aftermath of the 1996 election, factions formed within Perot's new party and, after remaining largely uninvolved during the 2000 election, Perot broke from the party, which then basically fell apart.

Perot's eccentricities made him a frequent target of parody on *Saturday Night Live*, where his short, big-eared character was portrayed by Dana Carvey and, later, by Cherie Oteri. These portrayals usually depicted him as a crackpot and garnered more than a few laughs.

His contention that he temporarily dropped out of the 1992 race because of threats to his daughter's reputation from within the government possibly contributed to his reputation as an eccentric. He contended in the media that political insiders planned to use faked nude pictures of his daughter to ruin her wedding. He later demonstrated that he had a sense of humor over the media portrayal of him as a loony by dancing with his wife to the tune of Patsy Cline's "Crazy" during an election event.

But Perot is more than just another weird Texan. He is also considered a national hero by many because of his unflagging support of servicemen and women, particularly POWs. In 2005, he was presented with the Bob Hope Five Star Award for Distinguished Service to America. He has been honored with a number of other awards as well, including the highest award offered by the Department of Defense, the first ever Patrick Henry Award (given for outstanding service to one's country), and the first ever Raoul Wallenberg Award.

Whether an eccentric, a hero, or both, one thing is certain: H. Ross Perot is an unforgettable character.

Chapter 26

"Claytie"

Clayton Williams
1931-present

Name: Clayton Wheat Williams
Lived: 1931-present
Texas connection: Born in Alpine, Texas
Occupation: Oil and gas businessman
Claim to weirdness: He's a big fan of tacky humor
Tex-centricity Scale: 7 bad jokes (out of 10)

If there's one thing Texas has lots of, it's good ol' boys. To demonstrate his credentials during the 2000 Texas governor's race, Clayton Williams had this to say when asked by a reporter if he felt good about courting "the Bubba vote":

"Hell, I am Bubba."

So relates the author of *Claytie*, the Texas A&M University Press book about the one-time candidate for the Texas governorship. Mike Cochran wrote his book about a man he calls "one distinctive maverick," a man who rightfully takes his place within these pages.

Clayton Williams is a West Texas wildcatter-cum-oil-tycoon. The millionaire head of multiple successful businesses in West Texas became familiar to the rest of the state in 1990 when he squared off against Ann Richards in the governor's race that captivated an entire state and came to be known as "Claytie and the Lady." Listed among the *Forbes* 400 wealthiest Americans, Williams spent millions of his own money on his campaign and at one time led Richards by 20 percentage points. His large lead would evaporate by election night, however, and Treasury Secretary Richards would become the second female governor in Texas history after Ma Ferguson.

During the campaign, Williams made a number of notable gaffes, many of which contributed to a public image of him as a typical Texas good ol' boy. The most well-known of his mistakes involved a group of reporters he had invited to his ranch to watch him work cows. The idea was for him to prove that he was an honest-to-goodness working cowboy. The reporters arrived and a West Texas gulley-washer ensued, to which Claytie responded with a now infamous comment which compared the storm to rape. And I quote: "If it's inevitable, just relax and enjoy it."

In addition to that particular knee-slapper, Williams regaled reporters with stories about his youthful trips to brothels in Mexico. He also once refused to shake Richards' hand at a campaign event in Dallas. As a result of these faux pas and others, many voters came to see him as overly brash and unpredictable. In the end, most political observers felt that he had given away an election that was his to win, mainly because of his West Texas cowboy swagger and a perceived lack of sophistication.

Williams seems to have adjusted well to the outcome of the

election, making amends with Ann Richards prior to her death and returning to his West Texas business affairs to more than recoup the $8 million he spent on the campaign. There is little doubt, in the final analysis, that Williams is a talented businessman, and even less doubt that he is among the most interesting of Texas' colorful political characters.

Chapter 27

"Good Time Charlie"

Charlie Wilson
1933-present

Name: Charles Nesbitt Wilson
Lived: 1933-present
Texas connection: Born in Trinity, Texas
Occupation: U.S. Congressman
Claim to weirdness: The mirrors in his bachelor pad
Tex-centricity Scale: 5 Charlie's Angels (out of 10)

"Charlie Wilson Regrets Nothing" read the headline in *Time* magazine. That article appeared in December 2007, just fifteen days before the movie *Charlie Wilson's War* debuted to critical acclaim.

Who ever heard of Charlie Wilson?

Not many people, apparently. And yet, a movie was made about him. This came as a result of his role in the arming of the

Mujahedeen of Afghanistan against the invading Soviets. And as far as his lack of name recognition—that's exactly how he wanted it. The *Time* articles states, "What is truly mind-boggling about Wilson's extraordinary saga is that not one word of it leaked to the press. He credits this to the bipartisan spirit in Congress at the time. 'It never leaked because nobody wanted it to,' he says."

Charlie Wilson was a little known representative from Southeast Texas, known less for his politics and more for his quintessential bachelor pad in Washington with its "floor-to-ceiling mirrors," and for the beautiful women who made up his office staff and allegedly went by the title "Charlie's Angels." An investigation led by Rudy Giuliani was once conducted against Wilson, but the government dropped its charges against him and he celebrated with a "Beat the Rap" party.

While Wilson was busy partying and womanizing, however, he was also busy on the House Appropriations Committee upping the funding for the Afghan rebels from $8 million to over $750 million. The high point came when Stinger missiles arrived and the Mujahedeen were able to rid Afghanistan of Russian helicopters.

"Good Time Charlie," also known as the "Liberal from Lufkin," defied many of the stereotypes of Texas politicians in those days. He was progressive, pro-choice, and pro-equal rights. But, like some of the more conservative cowboy politicians from his home state, he was straightforward and plain-spoken. He once called prominent liberated woman Pat Schroeder "Babycakes" to her face (and yet they somehow became fast friends). He has admitted, meanwhile, to having been "reckless" at times while he was in office.

Above all, Wilson was a determined foe of Communism and of the Soviet Union in particular. His opposition to the Soviet Union was heightened after he read an article about thousands of refugees fleeing Afghanistan as a result of the Soviet invasion. Meanwhile, a Houston socialite named Joanne

Henning appealed to Wilson to do something about the bloody red invasion.

And Wilson did just that. First, he pushed through the appropriations necessary to buy weapons for the Afghans. Next, he personally travelled to Egypt with a Texas belly-dancer and worked with an Israeli arms dealer to buy weapons from Egyptian leaders.

Then, Wilson worked with a shadowy CIA agent named Gust Avrakotos to get the rocket launchers and the thousands of machine guns he had obtained in Egypt across the border from Pakistan and into Afghanistan, on the backs of mules.

When the Soviet Union pulled out of Afghanistan in 1989, the president of Pakistan said, "Charlie did it." Wilson was invited to the CIA's headquarters to celebrate.

And celebrate is something that Wilson knew how to do well.

Two years later the Soviet Union collapsed, and not long after that, Wilson retired from Congress. His partying ways eventually caught up with him and, as the movie about his exploits was set to debut, Wilson was back home in Lufkin, Texas, recovering from a heart transplant. He had permission from his doctor to attend the premiere, which he did, as always, with a beautiful woman on his arm—his wife Barbara.

Part 3
Strange Sports Figures

Texas is home to "America's Team," the Dallas Cowboys. It's also the inspiration behind the football book/movie/TV franchise *Friday Night Lights*. Texas is the former home of the NFL's all-time leading rusher, Floridian Emmitt Smith (we'll claim him) and is the birthplace of Major League Baseball's no-hit king, Nolan Ryan. Lone Star sports fans cheer for the Spurs, the Rockets, the Mavericks, the Cowboys, the Texans, the Rangers, the Astros, and the Stars—teams that have won Super Bowls, Stanley Cups, and NBA Championships. (We're still working on that World Series.)

Needless to say, sports are big in Texas. And I haven't even mentioned golf—with luminaries like Ben Crenshaw, Tom Kite, Ben Hogan, Byron Nelson, Lee Trevino, and the incomparable Babe Zaharias heralding from the Lone Star State—or tennis, or NASCAR, or the ever-popular rasslin'.

They say everything is bigger in Texas, but it's quite possible that nothing is bigger in Texas than sports. With all the sports figures who have passed through our fair land, it should come as no surprise that there have been a few individuals who are or were—I'm trying not to say "crazy" here because that would be rude—let's say unique. Yes, that's the word. The same state that gave us the perfectly straight-laced Nolan Ryan has also produced the borderline certifiable Dennis Rodman.

Every one of the folks mentioned in this section is or was at one time involved in athletic endeavors in Texas or else is originally from Texas. And every one of them embodies the barbecue-tinged eccentricity that only comes from one state that I know of.

111

Chapter 28

"The Bear"

Paul "Bear" Bryant
1913-1983

Name: Paul William Bryant
Lived: 1913-1983
Texas connection: Coached football at Texas A&M
Occupation: College football coaching legend
Claim to weirdness: Two words—Junction, Texas
Tex-centricity Scale: 4 fedoras (out of 10)

I know, I know—Paul "Bear" Bryant is generally identified with another state to the east of Texas, a place where the tide is apparently crimson. But Texas has a claim to this incredible coach, too, as he was the head football coach at Texas A&M from 1954 to 1957, just prior to his legendary stint at 'Bama. In fact, it was while leading the Aggies that Bryant coached his one and only Heisman Trophy winner, running back John

David Crow. Bryant compiled an impressive 25-14-2 record while at A&M, and he also established himself firmly in the canon of Texas football lore with a trip to a little place called Junction.

We'll return to Junction shortly. First, a bit of a bio.

Bryant was born in Alabama (Moro Bottom, to be precise), the 11th of 12 children. Legend holds that he earned his nickname at the age of 13 after agreeing to wrestle a live bear. No word on whether or not he actually wrestled the bear, but if he did, he did not apparently die.

After high school, Bryant excelled on the University of Alabama football team. He was drafted in the 4th round by the pros but chose to go into coaching instead. His assistant coaching career took him to Union University, the University of Alabama, and Vanderbilt. His first head coaching job was at North Carolina Navy Pre-Flight, followed by stints at Maryland, Kentucky, Texas A&M, and finally Alabama.

At one point right after the Japanese bombing of Pearl Harbor, Bryant was offered the head coaching job at the University of Arkansas. He opted instead to join the Navy and saw battle on the *USS Uruguay*. According to the author of *The Last Coach: The Life of Paul "Bear" Bryant*, Bryant once defied orders to abandon ship after the *Uruguay* was rammed; as a result he saved the lives of many men.

His reputation as one of the greatest coaches of all time is well-deserved, and he earned it largely at Alabama. At that school, he won six national titles and even more Southeastern Conference championships. When Bryant retired he was the winningest coach in college football history.

But we aren't here to talk about Alabama, are we? We are here, my friends, to talk about eccentricities performed within the boundaries of or for the honor and glory of the shining Lone Star State. And few eccentric flourishes are more proudly recounted by those affected by them than the episode that took place under the blazing sun in Junction.

Bryant was not, shall we say, a touchy-feely coach. He was intense. Hard-nosed. Tough.

He *was* football.

And when he told the Aggies to get on the bus, he meant business. The team he had inherited, one which he felt lacked discipline and toughness, was headed to the Texas A&M adjunct campus at tiny Junction, Texas. At that particular time, Junction was well into year four of a six-year drought, the worst in its history. The boys were at Junction for ten days, and the temperature topped 100 degrees on every one of those ten days.

One wonders if any of those Aggies were asked to write a paper entitled, "What I Did During My Summer Vacation" when they went back to school in the fall. Had a teacher assigned that, many of the players could have summed things up in three short words: "I almost died."

Bryant did not take pity on the players, despite the harsh climate. He scheduled a brutal practice regimen for them while in Junction, and he refused to let them take water breaks.

That's right, no water breaks.

Believe it or not, no one died. One survivor reported later in life that he lost ten percent of his body weight in sweat in a single day. Others reported that the only relief afforded them was a single wet towel to be shared among the offensive players, and another for the defense.

The numbers dwindled daily. By the end of day ten, Bryant was left with a fraction of the number of players he had started with. The number of those who remained varies depending on who's telling the story—it was either in the upper 20s or lower 30s.

The "Junction Boys," as they came to be called, went 1-9 that year. But success was in the offing. Two years later, they beat the University of Texas Longhorns for the Southwest Conference title, their first title in years. Many credited the torturous camp at Junction for bringing together a team that could overcome great odds and become winners in such a short time.

Coach "Bear" Bryant was known for his ever-present fedora, his quiet demeanor, and his intense approach to football. He was possibly a little bit sadistic. Despite these personality quirks, however, he is remembered as one of the most successful and, believe it or not, most beloved coaches in college football history. As an example of the respect his players had for him, he was given a prize possession—the ring he was buried with—by the "Junction Boys" he had abused and turned into men.

And since there isn't a book called *Alabama Eccentrics* as far as we know, we've chosen to include this noteworthy one-time Texan in the pantheon of audacious Lone Star characters.

Chapter 29

"The Maverick"

Mark Cuban
1958-present

Name: Mark Cuban
Lived: 1958-present
Texas connection: Lives in Dallas, Texas
Occupation: Owns the Dallas Mavericks; chairman of HDNet
Claim to weirdness: The bad hair
Tex-centricity Scale: 6 NBA fines (out of 10)

Mark Cuban would fit just as nicely in the chapter about businessmen. He is a self-made billionaire, after all. The former Dallas bartender and Indiana University graduate created a little startup company so he could listen to Hoosier basketball while living in Dallas, and it quickly morphed into Broadcast.com, a highly-touted tech firm that Cuban and a partner sold to Yahoo! for over $5 billion in 1999. His other business interests have included a movie distribution company, Landmark movie theaters, and HDNet, the first high-definition cable television network. He has also invested heavily in a variety of new tech firms.

But we—"we" meaning "I"—chose to include Cuban in the sports section because, a.) the section's too short without him, and b.) he's a HUGE sports fan. It has been said that he is living every fan's dream. Not only is he a fan; he's also a major sports businessman, with varied interests in several sports.

Let's start with the most visible of his sports investments. One of the first moves Cuban made after becoming ridiculously rich was to purchase the NBA's hapless Dallas Mavericks from H. Ross Perot, Jr. And, as any NBA fan can tell you, the move was great for the Mavericks. Cuban has been one of the most involved (and one of the most animated) of NBA owners during his time in the luxury suite. Only, he doesn't sit in the owner's seat. He sits in the bleachers with the other schmucks, cheering and acting crazy. The Mavs number one fan also installed television sets and video game systems in the locker room and generally made life as a Dallas Maverick a good thing. And he brought in great players. The end result of all this was that the perennially-losing Mavericks have become winners. They won over 50 games the year after Cuban purchased the team for $285 million. Only two years prior, the Mavericks had won only 14 games in a strike-shortened season.

As an owner, Cuban has garnered a reputation as a winner, but also as something of a, well, maverick. His NBA fines have totaled well over one million American dollars, mostly for criticizing referees. He has also earned criticism for audacious moves such as bringing NBA bad boy (and fellow eccentric) Dennis Rodman to Dallas and even allowing The Weird One to live in his own house for a while. He turned criticism into national press attention in 2002. After saying the NBA's manager of officials wouldn't be able "to manage a Dairy

Queen," Cuban agreed to spend two hours working behind the counter at a Dairy Queen in Coppell, Texas.

He has also garnered a reputation for bad hair. No statistics are available regarding the number of basketball fans who, while watching the Mavs play, have muttered, "With all his money, seems like he could afford a decent haircut." I can attest that the number is at least one, given the fact that I reiterate that very line each and every time Dr. Cubanstein's mug appears on the small screen. He joins Donald Trump as a card-carrying member of the BHCB—the Bad Hair Club for Billionaires.

But there's more to Mark Cuban than basketball and bad hair. Cuban has invested his money in other sports enterprises, too. He has been associated with efforts to buy the NHL's Pittsburgh Penguins, MLB's Pittsburgh Pirates and Chicago Cubs, and a Las Vegas franchise in the nascent United Football League. He has also launched a mixed martial arts organization on his cable network designed to compete against the Ultimate Fighting Championship. He even participated in a WWF professional wrestling match at one point, for some obscure reason.

Obviously, as the first major investor in an upstart professional football league, Cuban is in possession of a pretty wide contrarian streak. He has ponied up $30 million to be a UFL team owner despite that fact that the last three football leagues that tried to compete with the NFL—the USFL, the World League of American Football, and the XFL—have all folded like an old dollar bill, and that despite heavy investment from individuals and, in the case of the XFL, from major corporations. But Mark Cuban is undeterred.

Like Texas-based political oddball Ron Paul, Mark Cuban goes his own way. Also like Paul, Cuban was greatly influenced by the writings of Ayn Rand. When asked about Rand's novel *The Fountainhead*, Cuban says, "I don't know how many times I have read it, but it got to the point where I had to stop because I would get too fired up."

Cuban is a true pioneer in many ways, unafraid to venture into new territories and take big risks. He has certainly broken the mold for NBA owners with his populist antics in the bleachers, with his outspoken blog postings, and with his uninhibited criticism of foes including referees and even fellow bad-hair-billionaire Donald Trump. He's audacious; he's quirky; he's young and rich and funny.

And I just can't figure out, with all his money, why he doesn't get a better haircut. Pro-Cuts charges like ten bucks.

Chapter 30

"Big George"

George Foreman
1949-present

Name: George Edward Foreman
Lived: 1949-present
Texas connection: Born in Marshall, Texas
Occupation: Pro boxer; pitchman
Claim to weirdness: Named all five of his sons "George"
Tex-centricity Scale: 6 KOs (out of 10)

There are crazy people who make you shake your head, and then there are crazy people who make you smile. George Foreman is of the latter class of crazy people. He's happy-go-lucky, he smiles all the time, and you never know what he'll say or do next.

The story of George Foreman is an unlikely one, to say the least. We all know how his story is supposed to turn out. It is supposed to go like this: young hotshot boxer becomes world champion. Rides the wave of fame for awhile, makes big bucks and bad decisions. Spends all his money on bad friends and drugs. Follows that road to its sad end. You meet him later in a bar somewhere and he tries to tell you about his glory days, but his mind is gone and you can't understand a word he says. Later, you read that he's in jail, a shadow of the man they used to call champ.

But George Foreman doesn't do things like everyone else. His unlikely path starts out on the streets, committing petty crimes and getting into trouble. It takes him to a boxing gym and leads to Olympic gold and a world heavyweight title. Nothing unusual so far. We've all heard that story a million times. And we know where it goes from there.

But this time we don't. From there it diverges wildly from the norm. Big George gives up drinking and smoking. He becomes a preacher, and he preaches every Sunday. His mind stays sharp. His speech remains clear, lucid even.

Then, when he is *way* past his prime, he revives his boxing career and fights the big names. He wins a world championship at age 45, two decades after he had lost the same belt to Muhammad Ali. He becomes a darling of boxing fans for the courage and determination he displays on the comeback trail, and he lands gigs as a boxing analyst and a television pitchman for a variety of companies. Some boxers his age can hardly talk—meanwhile, Foreman becomes a professional *spokesman*.

The former champ published two books and for a time had his own sitcom, "George," on ABC. To top it all off, in a venture that Foreman says has earned him more money and fame than he made in his entire boxing career, he became the name and the face of a popular grilling device, The George Foreman Lean and Mean Fat Reducing Grilling Machine.

From street thug to boxing phenom to preacher to middle-aged boxing phenom to kitchen appliance mogul, Foreman has lived a unique and satisfying life. And along the way he has been patently unafraid to be different.

Eccentric, you might even say.

Dare-to-be-different exhibit number one: of Foreman's ten children, five are boys. Of those five boys, five are named George. That's right. He named all of his sons George— George, Jr., and Georges III thru VI, to be specific. He also has a daughter named Georgetta.

Dare-to-be-different exhibit number two: in the same Olympic Games that saw two African-American runners stand on the medal platform and raise their fists in protest against conditions in the United States, George Foreman took an American flag and ran around the ring with it after his gold- medal winning knockout. This was not a totally popular decision at the time, and he was criticized by some. He made it clear, though, that he was proud to be from the USA. George Foreman did his own thing.

And George Foreman still does his own thing. Even though there are six George Foremans in his immediate family, Big George is truly one-of-a-kind.

Chapter 31

"The Renegade"

Charles Haley
1964-present

Name: Charles Lewis Haley
Lived: 1964-present
Texas connection: Worked in Dallas
Occupation: Former professional football player
Claim to weirdness: Came to Dallas with a reputation as an unpredictable hothead
Tex-centricity Scale: 3 quarterback sacks (out of 10)

No one has more Super Bowl rings than Charles Haley's five. He came to the Dallas Cowboys in 1992 wearing two of them. He also came with a reputation for cantankerous behavior. After he arrived in Dallas, Haley contributed his considerable talents to the victorious Super Bowl teams of 1992, 1993, and 1995. To this date, Haley still holds the record for sacks in Super Bowls, with 4.5. In addition, he recorded over 100 sacks in his career, and he was named Defensive Player of the Year, twice.

When he arrived in Dallas, lots of Cowboys fans expected the worst. Would this hothead from the evil San Francisco 49ers destroy the chemistry that had turned the Cowboys into contenders? Haley quickly proved the naysayers wrong, demolishing opposing offenses with a quiet intensity and staying out of trouble off the field.

After retiring from pro football in 1996 due to injuries, Haley reemerged briefly in 1998 and 1999 on the San Francisco 49ers roster. He went into coaching after that. Now, his name pops up regularly when football talk turns to Hall of Fame nominations.

Not the strangest cat in this book, for sure, but Charles Haley was a captivating character for the storybook Dallas Cowboys of the early- and mid-1990s. He subtitled his memoirs *The Life of an NFL Renegade*. And this renegade takes his rightful place among the other mavericks, rebels, and nonconformists in these pages.

Chapter 32

"Stout"

"Stout" Jackson
1890-1976

Name: Thomas Jefferson Jackson
Lived: 1890-1976
Texas connection: Born in Perrin, Texas
Occupation: Professional strongman
Claim to weirdness: Traveled the world lifting heavy things
Tex-centricity Scale: 6 feats of strength (out of 10)

Thomas Jefferson "Stout" Jackson's logo showed him sitting on a medicine ball, his legs pressed against two planks jutting out of the ground, leaning back and holding tight to reins. On the other end of the reins were two thick draught horses, straining in the opposite direction.

Tug of war with horses was just one of Stout Jackson's many feats of strength. He was also known to bend sixty-penny nails, break ropes, drive nails into boards with his fist, and pull cars with his teeth. He even occasionally boxed and wrestled. The feat of strength that landed him in the Ripley's "Believe It or Not" newspaper column was a reported 1924 back lift of 12 bales of cotton weighing 6,472 pounds. (*The Guinness Book of World Records* doesn't recognize this lift—it recognized Paul Anderson's back lift of 6,270 pounds as the best ever for several years, but then stopped recognizing that one after reviewing the supporting data and finding it insufficient.) Jackson's lift is not widely accepted by sports historians because much of the supporting documentation has since been lost, and strongmen of the early 20th century were prone, if you can believe this, to exaggeration and showmanship.

The back lift was Jackson's bread and butter. He back lifted bricks; he back lifted ten men, sometimes twenty. A back lift consists of a person stooping under a table-like platform laden with weight of some kind and straightening his legs, thereby raising the platform off of its supports. Many strong men have used this lift through the years.

Jackson was born on the Lasater Ranch just outside of Perrin, a North Texas town of 500 people that needs something to be famous for. His father was a Baptist preacher and a rancher. Jackson would frequently attribute his impressive strength to the healthy habits he developed during childhood, along with the demanding chores he performed. Despite his strength, Jackson was not a large man. In fact, he started the exercise regimen that would eventually lead to a career as a professional strongman after other children teased him and called him a "runt." After he had started exercising, his father took him to a circus and he saw his first strongman. He went home and, with a little practice, found that he could perform every feat he had seen at the circus.

At the age of 17, Jackson was ready to perform for an audience. When he assured his preacher father that he would use his show to tout the benefits of right living, his parents supported him in his endeavor. He gave his first show in the small town of Joplin, just up the road from Perrin. According to an article in *Iron Game History* by Kimberly Beckwith, Jackson charged fifteen cents a head at his first show and made an impressive total of $15.15 in one day—big money in those days. Soon he began travelling around the state. His father provided a wagon and a team of mules, and the young man took his show on the road.

He billed himself at different times in his career as "The Stoutest Man Living," "World's Greatest Strong Man," and the "World's Strongest Strong Man." For many years, Jackson offered to pay $1000 to a person in the audience who could out-strongman him. Jackson later claimed that he never had to pay. He also claimed that he had never been sick even one day in his life and had never suffered a single cavity.

Jackson's career as a strong man would last until his retirement in 1935. Before hanging up his silk shorts, Jackson took his show all over the U.S., Canada, and even into South America. He toured on his own, then with his wife and son, eventually buying a Model T. He also traveled with a number of circuses over the years. During the height of his career, Jackson bragged that he sometimes made $1000 in a single day by putting on multiple shows at county fairs.

Jackson's retirement came as his touring strongman business was slowing in the midst of the Great Depression. He settled in Robstown, Texas, and soon found himself involved in another trade. He noticed a lack of entertainment options for the Mexican-Americans in South Texas. These people (they called themselves Tejanos) were migrant workers who moved with the crops. They were often subjected to discrimination in a variety of services, including housing and education.

And, as Jackson noticed, in entertainment.

Jackson bought several large circus tents and started showing Spanish language movies. This was a natural outgrowth of his travelling strongman show: Jackson had long shown silent movies in a tent as a sideshow at his events.

Tejano families were often quite large and there were few affordable entertainment options available to them. Jackson's cheap ticket prices drew Spanish-speaking families in droves. They walked from surrounding communities carrying torches and flashlights. Charging ten cents for children and fifteen cents for adults, Jackson soon generated enough capital to expand his operation. A Texas state historical marker about Jackson's Carpas theaters ("carpas" is Spanish for tents) has this to say:

> Tejano workers and their families flocked to the theaters. Jackson showcased prominent Mexican and other Spanish-language entertainers, who would appear at the carpas in conjunction with screenings of their films. He also arranged for variety acts and occasionally Anglo performers would appear.

> After World War II, Jackson began to build permanent homes for his theaters. Based on tubular steel and concrete, his designs were structurally sound and resisted weather, vandalism, and even fire. Jackson also designed drive-in movie screens, fireproof housing, and bomb shelters. The last Teatro Carpa closed in 1963, its time run out as legal racial segregation came to an end.

Jackson's movie tents were so successful that he expanded to a number of Texas towns. The permanent structures he eventually built to house the theaters could seat thousands and sometimes doubled as makeshift hotels for travelers who, because of their skin color, were not allowed inside local hotels.

But the Jacksons didn't just make money from the Tejanos. Stout and his wife Beatrice evolved into local humanitarians.

Beatrice was a midwife for hundreds of Tejano mothers; it is said that many little girls in the Robstown area were named after her during those days. She made cloth-lined coffins out of cardboard boxes for mothers who lost their babies and couldn't afford anything else. In times of need, the Jacksons allowed Tejanos to use their telephone, one of the first in the county. Stout himself sometimes bailed Tejanos out of jail, and he sometimes helped gifted Tejano students pay for their schooling.

Eventually, Jackson turned his attention toward building drive-in movie screens, but his timing was bad as television had invaded the American home and would soon doom the drive-in movie. Jackson made a short-lived comeback as a strongman in his late 50s. He found that he could still perform most of the feats of strength he had done in his youth, and he did a small number of shows around South Texas. He lived the rest of his days out quietly and died in an Austin retirement home in 1976.

Thomas Jefferson Jackson, aka "Stout," was a unique character in Texas history. A showman, a strongman, an entrepreneur, a humanitarian, and even an inventor (Jackson registered a number of patents for his building techniques). Jackson is well-remembered in a portion of South Texas as a larger-than-life figure who in 1924 very well may have lifted more weight at one time than any man before or since.

Chapter 33

"Crazy Ray"

"Crazy Ray" Jones
1931-2007

Name: Wilford Jones
Lived: 1931-2007
Texas connection: Lived in Dallas
Occupation: Dallas Cowboys' #1 fan
Claim to weirdness: Zany ballgame antics
Tex-centricity Scale: 7 stick horses (out of 10)

Every person in this book is unique, but no other eccentric listed has had the audacity to select "Crazy" as his or her first name. Not so with the late Wilford Jones, better known by generations of Dallas Cowboys fans as the one and only Crazy Ray.

Crazy Ray was the Cowboys' unofficial mascot for many years. He started his career as a vendor, but he quickly endeared himself to fans as much more than that with his spirited cowboy outfits, stick horses, and colorful clowning around. While he was never officially employed by the Dallas Cowboys, Crazy Ray is said to have only missed three home games. And though he was never on the Cowboys payroll, he was given a few pretty sweet perks: free parking, an all-access pass to Texas Stadium, tickets to Super Bowl games, and a little financial help along the way from Cowboys owner Jerry Jones.

Crazy Ray's health declined steadily in the late 1990s and early 2000s. His leg was amputated at the knee because of diabetes complications, then glaucoma claimed his eyesight. He had four strokes and five bypass operations. He fell on financial hard times because of his health problems and those of his wife. His house began to deteriorate. His lights and water were shut off. On one occasion, he was found by a Good Samaritan wandering down a Dallas street disheveled and disoriented.

A neighbor and friend started a website, www.savecrazyray.com, which accepted donations to help Crazy Ray. Donations through the site helped to pay off the mortgage on Crazy Ray's modest home; they also helped Ray get caught up on his mounting medical debts.

Even as his health waned, though, Crazy Ray still went to all the Cowboy home games.

Crazy Ray's antics were regularly seen on televised broadcasts of Dallas Cowboys games. He famously "fought" with the Washington Redskins fan/unofficial mascot, Chief Zee, and more than once pulled his pistol on his head-dressed rival. He mopped sweat from his bald head with opposing teams' pennants, and he once chased a New York Giant out of the end zone with his scooter. He did many other less visible things to make Dallas Cowboys games just a little more special for those in attendance: he pulled pennies from behind kids' ears, blew his famous whistle, and performed magic tricks.

When he sold peanuts in the beginning, he always tossed the nuts "in all manner of 'crazy' ways," according to one fan. Hence the name. Whatever it took to make people smile, Crazy Ray was ready to do it.

An article in the *Washington Post* called Crazy Ray "the godfather of superfans." After his death in 2007, dignitaries lined up to remember him. Even Chief Zee missed a Redskins game (for only the second time in nearly 30 years) to attend a ceremony held for him at Texas Stadium. "We became like brothers," said Chief Zee (real name: Zema Williams) of his one-time enemy.

In 2000, when Visa and the Pro Football Hall of Fame teamed up to select the biggest fan from every NFL franchise, the choice for Dallas was a no-brainer. Crazy Ray is enshrined in Canton, in the fans' section, which is just and right. He is also enshrined in the hearts of millions of Dallas Cowboys fans who remember his particular brand of craziness with a fondness that is hard to put into words.

Chapter 34

"The General"

Bobby Knight
1940-present

Name: Robert Montgomery Knight
Lived: 1940-present
Texas connection: Worked in Lubbock
Occupation: Texas Tech University basketball coach
Claim to weirdness: Temper tantrums are normal, but not at his age
Tex-centricity Scale: 9 dented chairs (out of 10)

Bobby Knight is proof that there is a vortex somewhere over Texas that sucks over-the-top characters irresistibly to the fair state's sandy climes. At any given time, you can look around at the world of sport and identify the goofiest, most off-the-wall person involved in a given sport, and you can know that it's only a matter of time before that person moves to

Texas. If they're weird, they'll find their way to Texas. From Deion Sanders to José Canseco to John Rocker, they always wind up here.

But back to Bobby Knight. Yes, he was at Indiana forever, but he wound up at Texas Tech, and that makes him eligible for this book.

Knight, also known as "The General" thanks to his authoritarian style of leadership, is famous for his ability to win college basketball games. He's also famous (or infamous) for his temper and his occasionally off-the-wall behavior. In terms of winning, Knight has notched more victories than any other NCAA Division I coach in history. He was named Big Ten Coach of the Year six times, and has furthermore earned Coach of the Year honors from the *Dallas Morning News, Basketball Times,* and the National Association of Basketball Coaches. He was named National Coach of the Year at one time or another by the Associated Press, United Press International, *Basketball Weekly*, and the United States Basketball Writers' Association; the Atlanta Tipoff Club has named him the Naismith College Coach of the Year. He has even been recognized on the floor of the Texas State Legislature. No word on whether or not he threw any of those chairs—I hope not—they're very heavy.

Knight's accolades are well-deserved. He has won one National Invitational Tournament (NIT) championship and three NCAA championships, and has led teams to the gold medal in the 1979 Pan-American Games and in the 1984 Olympic Games. He was the youngest coach ever to win 800 games, and is one of only four coaches to have ever done so. He led the Indiana Hoosiers to 11 Big Ten championships during his time there. He accomplished all this while never being sanctioned for recruiting violations, and according to one source, while maintaining a high graduation rate among his players—approaching 98%. The biography for Knight at the Texas Tech website had this to say: "In college basketball, the name Bob Knight is synonymous with greatness and winning."

Some might insert at this point that the name Bob Knight is also synonymous with temper tantrums. For all his success, Bobby Knight is, for many people, best known for his colorful and often controversial behavior.

In one well-known case, Knight threw a folding chair across the court during a game. In another, he put a loud-mouthed fan into a trash can during the Final Four. He was arrested in Puerto Rico during the Pan-American games for assaulting a police officer and was later convicted *en absentia*. He once brandished a bullwhip at practice, which most observers prayed was an attempt at satire. He wasn't joking, however, when he head butted one of his players and kicked his own son, who was playing for him at the time.

Knight was once filmed laying "a straight-arm Darth Vader chokehold on one of his own players," to borrow a vivid line from *Time* magazine's Lance Morrow. Soon after the neck-clutching episode, he manhandled another Indiana student and was subsequently fired from a school where he had compiled a 662-239 record over 29 years.

And the physical abuse that he doled out doesn't even compare to the taunts and sarcasm he has issued during his career. He has been accused of "motivating" players by putting tampons in lockers, directing racially-insensitive comments at minority players, and issuing forth a veritable fount of profanity.

And yet, most of his players love him in almost indescribable terms. The student body at Indiana protested after his ouster and posted signs that read, "Wanted: Dead" regarding the student whose allegations brought about "The General's" downfall.

Since coming to Texas, Knight has been involved in at least one noteworthy off-the-court episode. While dove hunting in Lubbock with a companion, Knight was confronted by a homeowner upset that the men were hunting too close to his house. A confrontation ensued, which the homeowner filmed, conveniently.

In another instance of strange behavior, Knight gave a press conference after winning his 899th game. He spoke to the gathered media with his 21-month-old grandson sitting on his lap. In the meeting, Knight used a bit of Texas-flavored profanity—known in semi-polite society by the call letters BS. (Knight didn't use the abbreviation, mind you). All the while, the little one looked on innocently.

Bobby Knight's antics have earned him the scorn of many in the press corps, which he has derided mercilessly, but the antics have also earned him the adoration of loyal basketball fans and players and even earned him his own short-lived reality show, ESPN's *Knight School*.

In an article for the *Washington Post*, John Feinstein writes, "People want heroes to be heroes and villains to be villains. It is rarely that simple and it isn't even close to being true with Knight." Bobby Knight is so thoroughly villainous in some ways, and in other ways so completely heroic, that he cannot be easily defined by frustrated sportswriters nor easily understood by sports gawkers. His audacity has paved the way to one success after another, but it has also led him to some deep, dark places. This complexity of personality makes him an unforgettable character. And like so many other unforgettable characters—from Davy Crockett to Martin Parmer to Judge Roy Bean—there came a time when Bobby Knight was drawn inexorably to Texas.

Some people speculate that the Bermuda Triangle is a magnet to mysterious energy forces. In much the same way, an argument might be made that Texas pulls in the eccentrics of the world through some cosmic force, as yet unidentified, possibly proceeding forth from the Barnett Shale or the rocky outcroppings of the Davis Mountains. It draws them in like mosquito hawks to a bug zapper, but instead of frying them to a crisp, the Lone Star State frees their inner lunatic and allows them to achieve even greater bizarreness than they ever thought possible.

And something tells me that, despite his retirement from coaching in 2008, we haven't seen the craziest thing Bobby Knight has in store for us yet.

Chapter 35

"The Mastermind"

Mike Leach
1961-present

Name: Michael C. Leach
Lived: 1961-present
Texas connection: Works in Lubbock
Occupation: Coaches the Texas Tech University football team
Claim to weirdness: The pirate fixation
Tex-centricity Scale: 8 eye patches (out of 10)

The athletics department of Texas Tech University apparently has an affinity for wacky characters. Not only did they hire the notorious Bobby Knight to head up their NCAA basketball program, but they also obtained the services of one Mike Leach to lead their football team.

It's not that Leach isn't a good coach. He is, by many accounts, an offensive genius. A guru of Yogian proportions. A mastermind of moving the American football down the American football field.

But for all his success on the football field, he's one weird dude.

Consider first of all his history. Mike Leach is one of a very small handful of NCAA Division I coaches to have never played college football. In fact, he is quite possibly the only Division I coach to have never played a down of organized football period. (He rode the bench his junior year in high school and then called it quits.) Apparently, his physique bears out his athletic history: in an interview with the *New York Times*, one of the Red Raiders is quoted as saying, "When you first meet him, you think he's an equipment manager."

To his unique history we can add his tendency of fixating on quirky subjects. One season while coaching at Tech, Leach became a devotee of piracy and spent the entire off-season reading everything he could find on the subject. The next football season, his pre- and post-game speeches were full of references to pirates and exhortations for his players to do things like "Use your sword." (Their bodies were their swords.) Once, before a game against the Aggies, Leach looked at the Texas A&M cadets standing at attention in the stands and then wondered aloud to a journalist standing beside him, "How come they get to pretend they are soldiers?" He then proposed that students at Tech dress up like pirates and stand in the bleachers with bandanas and Jolly Rogers.

Then there's the motivational aspect to his game. Some coaches have gone down in history for their ability to stand in the locker room before a tough game or during a brutal halftime and deliver stirring oratory to light a fire in the bellies of their players.

Leach has a different approach. He bores his players *ad infinitum* with pedantic details and rambles until they want nothing more than to get out of that locker room. Tech's quarterback told the author of the *Times* article that he had

139

learned not to ask questions during locker room speeches because, when he does, the locker room lecture "just goes on longer."

Leach's eccentricity also shows in the Frankensteinian product he puts on the football field. And, in keeping with one major theme of this book, not everything that is weird is bad. Yes, Leach's offensive production is positively freakish; but, like a four-legged man in a butt-kicking contest, it's freakish in a good way.

Leach has turned a whole conga line of unheralded quarterbacks into legitimate stars. He broke offensive and passing records as an offensive coordinator at three colleges before being named head coach at Tech, and then his Red Raiders led the NCAA in passing yards four years in a row. Multiple Tech quarterbacks have sat atop the entire NCAA in passing yards. One, Kliff Kingsbury, broke the record for completions in a college career in only three years under Leach. This type of production has led to an amazing run of success at Tech which includes, as of this writing, a record of 65-37, along with a 5-3 mark in post-season play.

Leach has taken Texas Tech to a bowl game in every season he has been head coach, and he is among a very select group of college head coaches who have never had a losing season.

Unlike his infamous colleague on the Tech hard-court, Leach hasn't often courted controversy while in Lubbock. He has been content to court weirdness. Nevertheless, in 2007 Leach was fined a Big 12 record $10,000 for criticizing the officiating after a Tech loss to the University of Texas Longhorns. Leach had called the work of the referees in that game "a complete travesty." He later seemed unfazed by the fine, however, dismissing it by noting that his team was used to setting records.

Like Bobby Knight, Mike Leach seems to have found a home in Lubbock where he can be himself. With a five-year contract paying him $10 million through 2010, he can probably afford a few more record-breaking fines. And he can indulge his passion for pirates as much as he wants, as long as his players keep "passing the ball as soon as they get off the bus," as one sportswriter has put it. Because in Texas, if you're crazy and you're losing, you're just crazy. But if you're crazy and you're winning, you're just a winner.

Chapter 36

"T. O."

Terrell Owens
1973-present

Name: Terrell Eldorado Owens	
Lived: 1973-present	
Texas connection: Works in Dallas	
Occupation: Professional football player	
Claim to weirdness: His oversized ego	
Tex-centricity Scale: 6 touchdown celebrations (out of 10)	

Terrell Owens has courted controversy from the time he first put on a National Football League uniform. Drafted by the San Francisco 49ers, Owens came to prominence after Jerry Rice was injured in 1997. In 2000, Owens set the single-game receptions record by catching 20 balls in a game against the Chicago Bears. But Owens wasn't satisfied with catching balls and scoring touchdowns. It became apparent early on that he had an insatiable need for conflict and media attention. Maybe he didn't get the attention he needed when he was a toddler.

Owens' troubles in San Fran started with a series of highly-publicized spats with quarterback Jeff Garcia and head coach Steve Mariucci. I'm going to go out on a limb here and guess that Owens wanted the ball more. Owens then began his career-defining tradition of outrageous end zone celebrations, many of which have resulted in criticism, fines, and spectacular media coverage. In one instance, he mocked the Atlanta Falcons "dirty bird" dance, slashing at his throat while doing so.

In another, he celebrated a touchdown against the Dallas Cowboys by running to the star at midfield of Texas Stadium and dancing on top of it. Twice. (The second time he was sent sprawling by a Dallas defender, George Teague, who was ejected. Owens himself was fined and suspended by his team.) In another infamous celebration, Owens once pulled a Sharpie from his sock and signed a football after a touchdown. He celebrated another touchdown by borrowing pompoms from a cheerleader and performing a brief sideline routine.

In 2003, Owens left the 49ers after a lackluster season. He immediately lashed out at his former team in a national magazine.

Owens was received warmly by the fans of the Philadelphia Eagles when he arrived in that city in 2004, but the honeymoon wouldn't last long. He quickly wore out his welcome with his self-centered, anti-team antics. He wore a Dallas football jersey on the flight home from a game in which the Eagles lost to the Cowboys. When questioned by reporters, he said he didn't care what the fans thought.

He got into a fistfight with a retired Eagle in the Philadelphia locker room and later announced on his pre-game radio show that he wished he'd never signed with Philly.

His outlandish celebrations continued while in the City of Brotherly Love. He invented "The Bird Dance." He co-opted

Ray Lewis' pregame routine for an end zone celebration against the Baltimore Ravens. He pulled out a white cloth and served the football like a waiter after his 100th touchdown.

He tore a "T.O. has B.O." sign off the wall in Cleveland. And he dropped and did six sit-ups after his sixth touchdown of the season. During that same season, he starred in a controversial skit that aired on Monday Night Football in which an actress from *Desperate Housewives* dropped her towel and flashed him.

Owens crossed the line, however, when he criticized Philadelphia's immensely popular quarterback Donovan McNabb repeatedly, implying that the QB "got tired" in a playoff game and comparing him unfavorably with Green Bay's "warrior" quarterback Brett Favre. After these incidents, Owens was suspended for four games and benched the remainder of the season. This would end his one and only inglorious season in Philadelphia.

Four days after Owens was released by the Eagles, the very team he had disrespected by "dancing on the star" cheerfully signed him.

Months later, Owens was embroiled in controversy yet again after spitting in an opposing player's face. He was fined $35,000 for his actions. Never one to shy away from hatefulness, Owens made a point to praise Bill Parcells' replacement after the legendary coach retired; he failed to mention anything positive about the hard-nosed Parcells.

Owens' end zone hi-jinks for the Cowboys included pretending to take a nap with the football for a pillow; dropping a TD ball into an oversized Salvation Army kettle; and pretending to hide and use the ball as a video camera in the wake of the Bill Belichick spying controversy.

As of this writing, Terrell Owens remains a member of the Dallas Cowboys and, despite his flamboyant behavior, he remains popular with Dallas fans.

His popularity is due in large part to the success he has seen in a Cowboys uniform. In 2007, he broke the Dallas Cowboys' record for touchdown catches in a season. As of the end of the 2007 season, Owens was third all-time in touchdown receptions in the NFL, making him a very probable candidate for the NFL Hall of Fame.

More importantly, he is a shoe-in for the All Eccentric Team.

Chapter 37

"The Worm"

Dennis Rodman
1961-present

Name: Dennis Keith Rodman
Lived: 1961-present
Texas connection: Grew up in the Oak Cliff section of Dallas
Occupation: Retired pro basketball player, actor, former pro wrestler, professional weirdo
Claim to weirdness: Hair colors, wedding dresses, and general, deliberate wackiness
Tex-centricity Scale: 10 rebounds (out of 10)

Terrell Owens is a wallflower compared to this guy...
    Some people *are* weird, and some people *act* weird. Dennis Rodman acts weird. Very weird. And he has made a good living because of his unpredictable behavior. Well, to be fair, because of unpredictable behavior *and* because he rebounds a

basketball like a machine.

Rodman is a different kind of eccentric—more deliberate than most, you might say. You get the idea when you watch him on television decked out in a wedding gown (and it should be noted here that Dennis Rodman is in all likelihood the ugliest bride of all time) that this man is just *trying* to be outrageous. Granted, he has succeeded time and again at this ignoble goal, but you do feel something of a letdown when you realize that the train wreck you're watching has been staged.

Rodman's athletic credentials can't be overstated. He led the NBA in rebounding for seven consecutive years and was named the Defensive Player of the Year, twice. He was also a part of five championship teams during his pro career. And this after only lasting half a season on his high school basketball team in the Oak Cliff section of Dallas. As a youngster, the skinny 5'6" Rodman quit halfway through his first season after not seeing as much playing time as he wanted.

Rodman's trip to the NBA went through DFW International Airport, where he was a nighttime janitor until a friend told a community college coach about him. He had sprouted to 6'6" since graduating from high school and, after leaving the airport's night crew and bouncing from Cooke County College in Gainesville, Texas, to Southeastern Oklahoma State University, he became a three-time All-American.

Rodman's story would have made a great Hallmark Special if he wasn't so dang obnoxious. The janitor wound up being selected by the Detroit Pistons in the second round of the 1986 draft. He played tenacious defense for the Pistons for six years before playing two seasons for the San Antonio Spurs, three seasons for the Chicago Bulls, and partial seasons for the LA Lakers and the Dallas Mavericks. He followed these moves with stops in the ABA, the British Basketball League, and one game in Finland's Korisliiga.

As successful as Rodman the athlete has been, Rodman the showman is probably even more triumphant. In a few short years, he perfected his peculiar brand of self-promotion, parlaying his reign as the weirdest dude in basketball into a lucrative vocation as an offbeat entertainer and professional famous person. He became a household name by engaging in progressively more erratic behavior on and off the court with each passing year, and he continues to be remembered as one of the strangest athletes ever.

Rodman, also known as "The Worm," accomplished several lowlights during his basketball career. For example:

1. He insinuated that Larry Bird was overrated because of his skin color
2. He frequently engaged in on-the-court arguments with other players
3. He kicked a courtside cameraman in the groin (and paid a $200,000 settlement)
4. He constantly dyed his hair with bright colors and wild designs and covered his body in tattoos
5. He head-butted a referee (for which he was fined and suspended)
6. He criticized Dallas Mavericks team owner Mark Cuban (and was subsequently cut from the team)

Rodman's off-court life was no less attention-grabbing. He entered into a high-profile relationship with Madonna, the pop music superstar, and later dated actress and full-time hottie Carmen Electra.

Nowadays, when he isn't cavorting with famous females, Rodman stays busy engaging in promotional activities. From the time he first became a household name to the present day, Rodman has lent his name recognition to a whole string of odd enterprises. He has served as commissioner of the Lingerie Football League, and he has participated in professional wrestling matches (once skipping practice with the Chicago Bulls in the process).

Rodman has acted in several poorly-received motion pictures and has appeared on the television sitcom *Third Rock from the Sun*, playing an alien. (In a similar vein, he was mentioned in the movie *Men in Black* as an alien-in-disguise.)

He wrote an autobiography and famously appeared in a white wedding dress to promote it. He has also participated in many basketball-related events around the world, shooting hoops in the Philippines, Finland, and England, and playing against the Harlem Globetrotters in his home country. Rodman appeared nude in an advertisement sponsored by People for the Ethical Treatment of Animals and has appeared on reality television shows in the U.S. and abroad.

Rodman has also had at least two reality shows of his own: MTV's *The Rodman World Tour* (1996) and HDNet's *Geek to Freak* (2007), in which Rodman tried to make overly prudish men and women into "edgy mavericks like himself," to borrow a line from his official website. In one scene from the show, Rodman helps an apparently uptight businessman become a drag queen. TV at its most dramatic and uplifting, I'm sure.

Rodman has also been involved in several legal dustups during and since his professional basketball career. In 2001, it was reported that his home was visited by local police some 70 times due to complaints from neighbors about boisterous parties.

Authorities also impounded his speedboat, as it was tied to another man's dock without permission. That same year, he reportedly sprayed a restaurant full of patrons with a fire extinguisher in response to someone saying something rude to him. (Apparently the people *around* Rodman aren't allowed to be outspoken.) No charges were filed.

Dennis Rodman finds himself in good company at the pinnacle of the Tex-centricity Scale, sitting alongside such luminaries of lunacy as "Silver Dollar" Jim West and Stanley Marsh 3. Like them, Rodman is a showman, calculating in his oddities and raking in the proceeds from his provocative lifestyle. And most onlookers almost certainly realize as much, but yet, even though we know that the train wreck is staged, we just can't make ourselves look away.

And "The Worm" is counting on us to keep watching.

Chapter 38

"The Patriarch"

Fritz von Erich
1929-1997

Name: Jack Barton Adkisson
Lived: 1929-1997
Texas connection: Born in Jewett, Texas
Occupation: Pro wrestler
Claim to weirdness: The von Erich Curse
Tex-centricity Scale: 4 Iron Claws (out of 10)

Fritz von Erich—real name Jack Adkisson—shot to fame in the 1950s as a professional wrestler. A football player of impressive stature at Dallas' Southern Methodist University, Adkisson played one year for the NFL's Dallas Texans and then ventured north to the Canadian Football League. While in Edmonton, he became the character Fritz von Erich, an imposing Nazi sympathizer, after signing with the Klondike

Wrestling Organization. Von Erich gained fame in the United States and Japan and traveled to wrestling rings around the world. But his greatest fame would come later, when he and his sons evolved into wrestling royalty and ruled the sport from the Dallas Sportatorium in the early 1980s.

Fritz von Erich's signature move, one he would pass on to his sons, was known as the "Iron Claw." He would take one of his massive hands and spread out the fingers, holding the claw high in the air for the fans to see, and then he would clamp his phalanges hard onto his opponent's forehead, squeezing thumb and middle finger onto the other man's temples with all his might.

Von Erich would grimace with the effort; his opponent would often scream in agony. This move caused extreme pain, or at least the illusion of it. Oftentimes, the "Claw" was accompanied by blood streaming inexplicably down the opponent's face. Maybe von Erich needed to trim his nails.

By the 1980s, von Erich had morphed from wrestler to owner of World Class Championship Wrestling (WCCW), a major wrestling promotion based in Dallas. It garnered a huge viewership for several years on channel 11. The most popular wrestlers entering the ring each Saturday night were Fritz' sons: David, Kevin, Kerry, and later, Mike.

I remember watching wrestling on Friday nights like it was yesterday. I don't know who liked it more, me, my sister, or my dad. I just know we didn't miss it. And we all had our favorite von Erich. Mine was Kevin; I still vividly recall the time the von Erichs and their mortal enemies the Freebirds came to Jacksboro, Texas, just up the road from our hometown, and my dad took my sister and me to see them wrestle. It was crowded in the metal building where the bouts took place and it felt as if it was two hundred degrees inside. I wanted to leave, I remember, and I think my dad did too...but we stayed until David and Kevin von Erich had both won their matches against the bad guys.

I remember the time, too, that my mom and dad got out a tape recorder while we were all wrestling in the living room. We each took on a wrestling identity and conducted interviews into the tape recorder. My mom was "Squirrelly Shirley." I don't remember the names my sister and my dad chose that night, but I remember my wrestling name well. I was "Erich von Kevin."

On the Friday night wrestling show from the Sportatorium, Fritz von Erich often came out and spoke in defense of his sons. I remember him as the gigantic old man with a deep, raspy voice, the father of Texas wrestling. I also remember him as the author of a Christian tract I once found lying on a coffee table in our living room. It was after reading that tract that I asked my mom what I needed to do to become a Christian. I would be baptized a few weeks later.

But the Fritz von Erich story is a tragedy if there ever was one. Some have speculated that the von Erich family must have been cursed.

Fritz lost his first son, Jackie, in 1959, while living and wrestling in Buffalo, New York. Jackie was walking to a friend's house and brushed against an exposed wire at a house that was under construction. The electrocution itself didn't kill him; instead, he was knocked unconscious and fell face-first into melting snow and drowned.

David von Erich, also known as "The Yellow Rose of Texas," was probably the most popular of the younger von Erichs. Other wrestlers have since said that if David had lived, he would have been the world champion. Sadly, David died in Japan during a wrestling tour in 1984. The von Erich family website says he died of a severe attack of gastroenteritis. In the aftermath of David's death, the von Erichs and the wrestling world did not mourn alone—they were joined by the entire Dallas-Fort Worth Metroplex.

In 1985, Mike von Erich almost died from toxic shock syndrome. He had apparently gotten sick after surgery on a shoulder injury he had suffered while wrestling in Israel. During his illness, Mike's temperature reached 107 degrees. Though he survived this scary episode, Mike would never be the same. He lost much of his body mass and would never regain it.

He would also struggle with drug abuse for the rest of his life. Prior to his illness, Mike had been a popular wrestler, having responded admirably when thrust into the spotlight following the death of his brother David. Sadly, he took his own life by overdosing on drugs in 1987, just two years after almost dying from toxic shock syndrome.

The youngest of Fritz von Erich's sons, Chris, committed suicide in 1991, the fourth von Erich son to die, and the second to die at his own hand. The von Erich website says that Chris suffered from asthma and had to take medicine that made his bones brittle. It also notes that, while his brothers were tall and athletic, Chris stood 5'6" tall and was slightly built. The family website says that Chris "suffered from broken bones in the ring due to his medication and was never able to enjoy the fame of his older brothers. Chris became frustrated and depressed after losing his brothers and [sic] his failures in the ring. He ended his own life on September 12, 1991, shortly before his 22nd birthday."

The next tragedy to befall the von Erich family would be Kerry's death in 1993. Kerry had had a serious motorcycle accident in 1984 that caused significant damage to his right leg. Kerry continued to walk (and, some say, wrestle) on the surgically-repaired foot before the bones had a chance to heal, and doctors had to amputate his foot.

He continued wrestling with a prosthetic, which caused him great pain. Kerry would struggle with substance abuse problems as a result of the accident and the subsequent pain he suffered. Despite the pain, Kerry von Erich won the championship belt from Ric Flair and held it for 18 days, just months after the death of his brother David. He also made it to the World Wrestling Federation by 1990, where he wrestled under the name "The Texas Tornado." While wrestling in this national organization, Kerry fought in numerous bouts on his prosthetic foot and continued to struggle with drug problems. In 1992, Kerry left the WWF and returned to Dallas to wrestle in a regional promotion; Fritz' WCCW had since folded.

After coming back to Texas, Kerry was indicted on a charge of drug possession. The year was 1993. He committed suicide the following day.

Jack Barton Adkisson, aka Fritz von Erich, was blessed with six sons, but by 1993, all but one had died. Fritz permanently left the world of wrestling after Kerry's death and lived a quiet life on his Denton ranch, tending to his real estate investments. He died in 1997 from cancer. This true Texas legend passed away quietly in his sleep.

The only surviving von Erich is Kevin, now over 50 years old and a grandfather. Kevin wrestled barefoot, unlike most wrestlers, and often flew from the top ropes. He has appeared in wrestling events as recently as 2005 and 2006 and now lives with his family in Hawaii.

Fritz von Erich was by all accounts a demanding, hard-driving father, and he created a legendary wrestling empire in Dallas, with his sons crowned as princes. The glory days of the von Erichs were truly magnificent—few men have known the kind of triumphs that Jack Adkisson knew in his life. But, from these dizzying heights would come one terrific fall after another. And few men have known the kind of pain that visited the man who became Fritz von Erich.

Part 4
Atypical Artists

It's hard to imagine things getting any more bizarre than they already are in the Lone Star State. But wait. You are about to enter the part of this book where weird meets weirder.

Texas—a state where strangeness is part of the norm, where it's considered perfectly normal behavior to pour a package of salty peanuts into one's Dr. Pepper and guzzle that baby down, lumps and all, with a side order of Moon Pies and a Chick-O-Stick—is home to *artists*. That's right—we aren't all horse ranchers and oil barons and chain-smoking beauticians. Some of us are drama teachers, bassoon-players, and glass-blowers. I'm not sure, but I would wager that there's even one Texas mime somewhere—probably lurking on lower Greenville Avenue in Dallas.

We have all kinds of art in Texas. Music is almost certainly the most widely-produced form of artistic expression in the Friendship State, but there's also sculpture, painting, performance art, you name it. We have Hispanic art, African-American art, Native American art, and boring old white people art.

There's ballet, which, apparently, some people pay good money to see. (Don't ask me.) There are more art museums in major Texas cities than you shake an armadillo at. Even the five or six people who enjoy modern art may find something to love among the piles of twisted metal at the Nasher Sculpture Garden in Dallas or, better yet, among the priceless paintings at "The Modern" in Fort Worth,

We've already seen that businessmen and politicians and athletes can be weird in Texas. And artists are weird everywhere. So what do you get when an artist lives in Texas? You get something like the duck-billed platypus of the human species. The Texas artist is a mish-mash of seemingly contradictory qualities all rolled up into one bizarre burrito. Imagine with me, if you will, a lady with blazing red hair and equally red lipstick, with purple silk scarves hanging off of her, beads and sequins sewn into abstract designs on an otherwise normal blouse, and a long wool thrift-shop coat with oversized buttons laying on top of the whole getup. Now throw on a felt cowboy hat with an eagle's feather and season her over-dramatic voice with a decided twang, and you've got it.

The Texas artist.

Or, in the interest of gender equality, imagine a man on hand-painted bike, a Texas flag billowing from the back fender, his hair a mess and a generous portion of stubble sprinkled across his chin. That's him. The Texas artist.

What we have here is something that words fail to describe—quite possibly the most disconcerting of all human beings. Imagine the lovechild of Johnny Depp at his artsiest and Tanya Tucker at her countriest. Or better yet, imagine the product of a forbidden rendezvous between Frida Kahlo and Larry the Cable Guy. Not a pretty picture.

The Texas artist. Yes, Virginia, such a thing exists. And I'm sure there must be such a thing as a French redneck too. It's only fair.

And now on to some real-life Texas artists. You'll notice that a majority are involved in music—and what else would you expect from a state that was the cradle of psychedelic rock in the 1960s and is currently in the grip of a popular musical style known simply as "Texas country," a style known for its clean folksy sound and smart, edgy lyrics? What else would you expect from a state whose capital is also known as "The Live Music Capital of the World"?

But you'll find more than music here. You'll read about the first American to be commissioned by hoity-toity French fashion house Hermés to design silk scarves; you'll also discover the international king of avant-garde theater—they're both from Waco, that hotbed of groundbreaking creativity, as you might have suspected. You'll learn about movie makers, actors, and painters. And every one of them, in one way or another, is bizarre and Texan, if that's not too redundant for you.

Chapter 39

"The American Eccentric"

Wes Anderson
1969-present

Name: Wesley Wales Anderson
Lived: 1969-present
Texas connection: Born in Houston, Texas
Occupation: Movie director
Claim to weirdness: He sometimes wears a monocle. No, really.
Tex-centricity Scale: 8 flawed characters (out of 10)

If I pay for a movie, I watch it. No matter how bad it is.
Except for *The Royal Tenenbaums.*

I tried to make myself finish it. The critics adored it. One review used the word "wit." This made me think it would be funny. Any minute now, I kept telling myself. Get ready to laugh.

I started praying about halfway through that Bill Murray would morph into Carl Spackler and start swinging a golf club at some flowers. And then it happened. In the midst of some depressing scene that almost certainly involved casual drug use and a "flawed but passionate" person wallowing in dysfunction, my wife called from the bedroom.

"Can you help me reorganize the closet?" she cried.

I jumped at the chance.

Anderson has made several other movies, including *Rushmore*, *The Darjeeling Limited*, and *Bottle Rocket*. All of them bear his trademark style, a style that non-movie-snobs may not fully appreciate. Even some critics have finally tired of Anderson's monotonous approach, with his bold color contrasts and frequent use of slow motion. Reviewer Kyle Smith of the *New York Post* called *The Darjeeling Limited* "a slow train to Dullsville that makes all local stops." An Associate Press critic called it "a self-satisfied exercise in style over substance."

At the same time, many critics have praised Anderson's early movies for their sensibility and their distinctive, instantly recognizable style. Martin Scorsese called Anderson "The next Martin Scorsese" after watching *Bottle Rocket* and *Rushmore*. (No word on whether Martin Scorsese thinks being the next Martin Scorsese is a good or bad thing. One can assume.)

Several commentators have contended that Anderson makes the same movie over and over. One especially adept movie reviewer used the phrase "aimless melancholy" to describe the tone of Anderson's creations. Despite the polarized opinions of him—either he's the greatest filmmaker ever to live, or else you just don't "get him"—Wes Anderson has found himself in the Hollywood "in" crowd. But no one has yet put him in the Hollywood "normal" crowd, if such a thing exists. A Slate.com article labels Anderson and a handful of other young filmmakers of his era "The American Eccentrics." Wes Anderson, for one, has earned this nickname.

While fashioning himself as a Generation X intellectual, an independent movie hipster perfectionist who preens over his movies and demands a role in every aspect of their making, he has also created a persona for himself of unflinching oddness. He dresses in "suits intentionally a few sizes too small" and first met his friend Owen Wilson while wearing duck-hunting boots and shorts. He has also, at least once, worn a monocle, which is once more than anyone in this century should.

One interviewer began an article about Anderson by writing, "It's hard to take seriously a man wearing blue-and-white striped slacks, a brown dress shirt, and a green blazer..." The odd wardrobe contributes to an overall appearance of ridiculousness that his flowing hairstyle and boyish face only exacerbate. Anderson's long red hair frames a pale, angular face that brings to mind another classic of American cinematography, *Revenge of the Nerds*.

Perhaps Anderson's greatest contribution to the art and science of Texas eccentricity isn't his appearance. It's his movies. It's the fact that, in each of his artsy-fartsy flicks, he has framed for public consumption characters that can be fairly described only as "quirky," "whimsical," and "stinkin' weird."

While other figures in this book are clearly eccentric, Anderson is the only one who comes across as an evangelical about it. He's an unabashed goof and he parades before the public a whole procession of goofs, many of them depression-inspiring, in an apparent attempt to sell moviegoers on the concept that the American experience involves a great deal of dysfunction and bizarre behavior. In an interview with Citypaper.com, Anderson says, "Honestly, I'm not making movies where I think, 'Let me see how weird this can be.'" Instead, he says that he and his colleagues ask, "How personal can we make it? How much of our own experience can we get into it?"

If that's where his movie ideas come from, I can only conclude that I'm glad I'm not Wes Anderson. Apparently, what makes his movies off-kilter is the fact that he and his colleagues are off-kilter.

Or maybe it all just boils down to this: maybe weird movies are made by weird people. Whatever the case, there is no doubt that Houston-born movie-maker Wes Anderson, darling of the young intellectual set and of people who love movies that "say something," is a Texas eccentric of the highest caliber. If his movies don't prove it, the monocle and duck-hunting boots do.

Chapter 40

"Baduizm"

Erykah Badu
1971-present

Name: Erica Abi Wright
Lived: 1971-present
Texas connection: Born and raised in Dallas, Texas
Occupation: Singer
Claim to weirdness: Eclectic music and strange baby names
Tex-centricity Scale: 6 head wraps (out of 10)

Erica Abi Wright changed her name to Erykah Badu as a rejection of the slave name she felt she was given at birth. Interested in music from a young age, Dallasite Badu exploded onto the music scene with her incomparably eclectic style in 1997, with the release of her first album, *Baduizm*.

Badu's music has been described as "cerebral." (That means "smart," for those of you who aren't very "cerebral."

You know who you are.)

Unique arrangements consisting of diverse musical styles have led her to be compared in one sentence to both Billie Holiday and the masters of old-school rap. Commentators desperate for a cubby hole for her have proposed the term "neo soul." You know you're different when they have to invent a category for you.

Badu's lyrics often reflect her personal philosophies and wildly progressive political ideas. Despite her uniqueness, Badu's experience and commentary appeal to a great number of listeners, as demonstrated by the fact that her albums have consistently gone platinum.

During her career, Badu's personal appearance has garnered almost as much attention as her music. Early on, she invariably appeared in public wearing a massive head wrap that made her look like an Afro-centric Marge Simpson. While the head wrap is no longer a constant companion, Badu is still widely seen as a highly distinctive individual. Her greatest flourish of creative weirdness has apparently manifested itself in the child-naming process. Her first child—born to Badu and fellow oddball Andre 3000, a singer for the band Black-Eyed Peas—was christened Seven. No, that's not a typo. It isn't supposed to say Steven; it's the number seven. Badu redeemed herself only somewhat by naming her next child after a noun. This child—born to her and rapper The D.O.C.—is legally known as Puma. (Hey, it beats Reebok, at least.)

Badu remains active in her community. She serves South Dallas through a non-profit organization she founded to bring the arts to the inner-city.

Unafraid to be different, Badu is also apparently unafraid to make a difference.

Chapter 41

"Gatemouth"

Clarence "Gatemouth" Brown
1924-2005

Name: Clarence Brown
Lived: 1924-2005
Texas connection: Spent his childhood in Orange, Texas
Occupation: Frank Zappa's all-time favorite guitarist
Claim to weirdness: The nickname, mostly
Tex-centricity Scale: 2 capos (out of 10)

Clarence Brown is underappreciated by the masses, a late guitar virtuoso who toured worldwide and released dozens of albums, but who nevertheless failed to become a well-known musician—or a wealthy one, for that matter. But being a starving artist alone does not qualify one for eccentric status.

What does, then? Well, in this man's case, it's his nickname. Brown became known as "Gatemouth" early in his career because of the deep voice that came out whenever he opened up to sing. I'm not sure what a deep voice has to do with a gate, but still. I couldn't resist including this Texas crooner and showman on the basis of his moniker alone.

Then there's the name of his first album, 1948's *San Antonio Ballbuster*. I'm not sure what "ballbuster" meant in 1948, but it almost had to be tasteless. That might explain why he didn't release another album until 1972. No fewer than 36 albums followed that one, and Brown developed a respectable following in the U.S. and abroad. In the 1970s he was a regular guest on the popular country music variety show *Hee Haw*. He recorded an album with *Hee Haw* host Roy Clark in 1979.

Before he made it onto the small screen, however, Brown's musical career took a bit of a detour. In the late 1960s he left Nashville for New Mexico and became a deputy sheriff. He didn't stay away from music long, however. By popular demand, he toured Europe a dozen times during the 1970s. And he never looked back, touring and releasing albums into the 21st century.

Brown was known for his guitar-playing, but he also recorded vocal tracks, fiddle tracks, piano tracks, and drum beats to go along with his legendary picking. Brown's music defied easy categorization, and his songs have been stuck with many labels, from jazz, to blues, to zydeco, to country, to swing. He sauntered among musical genres on his records easily, as if there was only one genre in existence, the one called "music."

Brown's last album, *Timeless*, was released in 2004, a year before he died of lung cancer, emphysema, and heart disease in his childhood hometown of Orange, Texas. (He had been evacuated from Slidell, Louisiana, earlier that year after his home was destroyed by Hurricane Katrina.)

The raspy-voiced Texas musician won several awards during his long and lustrous career, including the National Academy of Recording Arts and Sciences Heroes Award. In

2000, the *New York Times* called him "an American master." In addition to influencing many respected musicians, Brown is known as one of the first American guitarists to use a capo.

While "influential" might be a better adjective to use for Clarence "Gatemouth" Brown than "eccentric," his nickname alone places him firmly within these pages. Besides, if you didn't know about him, you needed to.

And now you do.

Chapter 42

"Parental Advisory"

The Butthole Surfers
1981-present

Names: Gibby Haynes, Paul Leary, King Coffey, and Nathan Calhoun
Active: 1981-present
Texas connection: Formed in San Antonio
Occupation: Musicians
Claim to weirdness: Hmm…where do I start?
Tex-centricity Scale: 10 hallucinogens (out of 10)

Many experimental bands exist primarily for the purpose of shocking and offending the general public, but few do this as effortlessly and as completely as the inappropriately-named Butthole Surfers. Their ubiquitous scatological references, their frenzied and violent stage shows, and their unabashed use of recreational psychedelic drugs have made them one of the most criticized bands in history.

Not that they care.

The weirdness started almost from the time the two founding members, Paul Leary and Gibby Haynes, met at Trinity University in San Antonio. Drawn together by their mutual weirdness and their fondness for music that no one else liked, the two men formed a band that would initially perform live under a different name at each concert. They did a song called "Butthole Surfer" and, when the song name was mistakenly announced by an emcee as their band name at an early concert, they became the Butthole Surfers. The name hasn't necessarily helped them, as it has been edited into a variety of barely-recognizable forms by newspapers, magazines, and record stores over the years.

The strangeness of this band is legendary and prolific. They have produced a long string of albums which, as is wont among the "I can be weirder than you" experimental music set, bear titles that make absolutely zero sense to the average person. The deliberately absurd album titles include *Locust Abortion Technician*, *Independent Worm Saloon,* and *Electriclarryland*.

Many of their songs have equally incongruous titles and words; their lyrics are often intentionally provocative. They are at times political, at times silly, at times vulgar, but always decidedly counterculture. One album didn't even have song names. Instead, each song was represented by a dirty cartoon.

What is most surprising, perhaps, is just how normal they almost were. Lead singer Gibby Haynes was captain of the university's basketball team when he met his future band mate; he also participated in debate and was named "Accountant of the Year" by the university. (And they say accountants are boring.) Haynes went on to work for an accounting firm for a short time before scrapping it all and following the natural weirdo impulse to go to California.

Meanwhile, Paul Leary dropped out of college with only one semester to go and followed Haynes to California. While there, they played a few gigs. In one concert, they impressed a music executive and eventually scored a music deal.

In the years since, the band has played all over the world and has released dozens of albums. They were signed to Capitol Records, a major label if there ever was one, in 1992. While they maintain a following, it is small; they have never achieved platinum status. Only one of their albums ever even went gold. Apparently, Butthole Surfer music is an acquired taste.

While many bands can easily compete with the Butthole Surfers when it comes to sales and perhaps even musical ability, few if any can compete when it comes to wanton offensiveness.

In a less-than-glowing biography of the Texas band found at TrouserPress.com, John Leland and Ira Robbins have this to say: "There are few experiences in this life that leave one feeling as sullied as a spin through the grooves of a Butthole Surfers record. Unlike so many nouveau scuzzbos, [the] Buttholes don't descend into the depths of squalor to make a point about the human condition—they just like it down there."

One of the great joys in compiling this book has been finding nuggets of bizarreness that far superseded the author's expectations. In the case of the Butthole Surfers, for all the vulgar nuttiness that their chosen appellation would lead one to anticipate, there is one surprising twist that may well qualify for the Grand Prize of Peculiarity.

Let me just parenthetically insert here that the driving force behind the Buttholes (pardon the inexcusable pun) is Gibby Haynes. His screaming vocals and songwriting contributions are both annoying and patently offensive in every way. In examining the abominable pile of refuse that his contribution to society amounts to, one is tempted to ask what kind of parents are responsible for this creature.

And therein we find the supreme strangeness.

If you were a child of television-watching age in the

Dallas-Fort Worth Metroplex between 1975 and 1996, you will remember that the kindest, most child-friendly, most sensitive and happy and courteous and completely and totally decent man in the world was a fellow in red and white pinstripes named, appropriately, "Mr. Peppermint." Mr. Peppermint's real name was Jerry Haynes—Gibby's dad.

Few things are odder than the fact that the man most notable for his magic striped cane and his interactions with puppets named Muffin the Bear and Mr. Wiggly Worm is responsible for the existence of a man whose contributions to the American experience include song lyrics like "Johnny was a little lesbian midget boy."

"Weird" just doesn't seem to go far enough to describe this one.

Chapter 43

"Poly Means Many"

Tim DeLaughter
1965-present

Name: Tim DeLaughter
Lived: 1965-present
Texas connection: Native of Decatur, Texas
Occupation: Musician
Claim to weirdness: The robes
Tex-centricity Scale: 7 theremins (out of 10)

Tim DeLaughter started out in the music business by forming Tripping Daisy, a relatively normal rock band. Well, as normal as possible for a band that has since been called "neo-psychedelic" and released an album called *I Am an Elastic Firecracker.*

Huh?

Anyway, if you thought that was weird, wait till you see

what came next. After Tripping Daisy disintegrated following the tragic death of its co-founder Wes Berggren, Tim started a new band, one that at highest count consisted of 28 musicians.

The Polyphonic Spree is a project that has allowed consummate artsy musician DeLaughter to experiment with more sounds than the five-piece Tripping Daisy. That's not to say that DeLaughter didn't squeeze lots of sounds out of his first band: members played lead and rhythm guitars, drums, dulcimers, Califones, keyboards, Mellotrons, Ace Tones, cellos, bass guitars, trumpets, and banjos, among other things. They were even known to play car tailpipes. But DeLaughter wanted more. And he got it with The Polyphonic Spree and its 10-person choir, twin keyboards, drums, viola, violin, flute, bass, guitar, trumpet, trombone, harp, French horn, pedal steel guitar, theremin (what?), and electronic effects.

An ambitious project, indeed. And one that has found some traction on the eccentric Texas music scene and beyond—the Spree has toured the world.

In an interview with an Australian website, DeLaughter explained why something as bizarre as The Polyphonic Spree was possible in Texas. "A lot of it has to do with the weather," DeLaughter explained, "It gets hot there, we get kind of crazy from the heat. And how wide open Texas is and how eccentric the people are there. It kinda has a weird cross of humans. They're real friendly and they're real crazy at the same time, and I think it adds a stimulating ingredient for someone who's an artist or musician."

As if the whole enterprise weren't already strange enough, DeLaughter has the group dress in flowing robes at concerts. The wardrobe gives give them the distinct appearance of a religious cult. To quote one wit, DeLaughter's band "gives the term 'cult following' a whole new meaning."

If it's a cult, it's a happy one. The music produced by this band has been described as "euphoric" and "tripped out," and has been compared with the upbeat music of the Beach Boys and the *Sergeant Pepper* album by the Beatles. As odd as the whole venture is, DeLaughter and company avoid the heavy-handedness of many "experimental" bands. Their songs are usually short and pop-infused, not long odes to an artsy band's own artistic artsiness. Somehow, DeLaughter manages to get two dozen people in robes to play snappy music that pop fans can actually enjoy.

That's definitely strange.

Now, turn up that theremin!

Chapter 44

"Shock Rocker"

Roky Erickson
1947-present

Name: Roger Kynard Erickson
Lived: 1947-present
Texas connection: Lives and plays in Austin
Occupation: Musician
Claim to weirdness: Shock therapy
Tex-centricity Scale: 10 legendary comebacks (out of 10)

Roky Erickson is a living legend in Austin, Texas, the co-founder of a psychedelic band that Janis Joplin almost joined. While with this band, the 13th Floor Elevators, Erickson wrote and sang an enduring 1966 single, "You're Gonna Miss Me." This was the only single that the 13th Floor Elevators ever saw make the national charts.

Erickson's mental problems and legal problems began soon

after that hit. He started hearing voices in his head, according to one biographer, and tried to drown them out by turning on several radios and television sets inside his apartment. During this time, Erickson and his band mates publicly endorsed the use of recreational drugs, including marijuana and LSD, and they eventually caught the attention of Austin police.

Erickson was diagnosed as a paranoid schizophrenic after babbling incoherently while onstage at a 1968 concert; he was admitted to a mental health facility. Then, following a 1969 arrest for possession of one marijuana cigarette, Erickson pled not guilty by reason of insanity. The effort to avoid jail time backfired; he was sent to the Rusk State Hospital for the Criminally Insane. He stayed there for three years.

Freed from the state hospital in 1972, Erickson eventually formed a new band, called Bleib Alien, later renamed Roky Erickson and the Aliens. The next 15 years were relatively uneventful for Erickson in terms of music, though in terms of bizarre behavior he stayed busy. He was once arrested for stealing his neighbors' mail and decorating his apartment with it, and in 1981 he briefly made the news by claiming that an alien from Mars had inhabited his body.

A revival of his music career began in 1991, when several influential alternative bands came together to produce a tribute album to Roky Erickson entitled *Where the Pyramid Meets the Eye*. The title was a reference to Erickson's famous answer when a questioner asked him to define psychedelic music: "It's where the pyramid meets the eye, man," he had said.

In 1995, riding the wave of renewed relevance, Erickson released a new album, and in 2001 his brother Sumner was granted legal custody of him. Things started to look up—Roky Erickson got effective psychological treatment during this time, and he also received legal help in trying to recoup royalties that he was due for his published works.

In the years since, a filmmaker has produced a documentary about him, he has put on his first full-length concert in many years, and he has performed in California, New York City, London, and Finland. He even started driving. Erickson is so well-known in Austin that fellow Texas eccentric Amy Miller Simmons sells a confection called "The Roky Erickson" at her Austin-based Amy's Ice Cream shops.

Erickson's story is one of perseverance in the face of difficulty, and one of humility rewarded. His relevance was noted when bands like R.E.M. and ZZ Top contributed to his tribute album. Erickson was surprised because he hadn't realized how influential his music was.

When describing Erickson's return from the edge of mental illness to "laid back" music stardom, *The Austin Chronicle's* Margaret Moser stated, "Call it a comeback – *the* comeback, perhaps."

Turns out Roky was right when he wrote his biggest hit: we did miss him. And now he's back.

Chapter 45

"Eclectic Guitars"

Fair to Midland
1998-present

Names: Darroh Sudderth, Cliff Campbell, Jon Dicken, Brett Stowers, and Matt Langley
Active: 1998-present
Texas connection: Founded in Sulphur Springs, Texas
Occupation: Musicians
Claim to weirdness: A debut album designed as a "creepy children's book"
Tex-centricity Scale: 5 high notes (out of 10)

Their website touts them as "one of the most idiosyncratic musical forces in the Lone Star State," and Daniel Lukes writing for *Kerrang!* calls their music "off kilter." *LA Weekly* writer Paul Rogers calls them "ultra-eclectic."

Fair to Midland is a unique creation: an art rock band that

blends keyboards and heavy metal, soaring, melodic vocals and crunching riffs, along with spasmodic stage performances, while remaining uniquely Texan (just check out their name). After self-releasing two albums and being dubbed by several observers as one of the best unsigned bands on earth, Fair to Midland finally found a home on Serj Tankian's Serjical Strike label. Tankian is a poet, activist, and progressive rock pioneer; he fronted the quirky rock powerhouse System of a Down in the late 1990s and early 2000s. Tankian heard Fair to Midland in concert in Los Angeles and was "blown away," immediately signing them to his oddball label.

With their operatic vocals and their obscure lyrics, Fair to Midland is often compared to artsy head-bangers like Coheed and Cambria, Tool, and Mars Volta. The lead singer's antics during live shows have drawn comparisons to Iggy Pop, one of the biggest freak shows in rock history. Despite the comparisons to others, however, the band, which consists of small town Texans Darroh Sudderth, Cliff Campbell, Jon Dickens, Brett Stowers, and Matt Langley, seems destined to stand on its own. By combining a variety of influences, they've found a unique sound that sets them apart.

Chapter 46

"The Duct Tape Messiah"

Blaze Foley
1949-1989

Name: Michael David Fuller
Lived: 1949-1989
Texas connection: Born in Marfa; lived and played in Austin
Occupation: Musician
Claim to weirdness: A duct tape fetish
Tex-centricity Scale: 10 friends' couches (out of 10)

Blaze Foley is admired by many musicians. Multiple Grammy winner Lucinda Williams has called him "a genius and a beautiful loser." In the liner notes to a Blaze Foley tribute album, Townes Van Zandt (whose own story appears later in this chapter) said that Foley had "only gone crazy once. Decided to stay."

Foley started out as a Baptist gospel singer in a group with members of his family; he later became a salesman at Sears for awhile. When he got bored with that life, he hit the road and made his way through Atlanta, Houston, and Chicago before arriving in Austin. Foley was homeless most of the time; he slept in the houses of friends and in bars. One biographer tells a story of him sleeping underneath a pool table during an eight-ball tournament. Every time someone made a shot, he would wake up and bang his head on the bottom of the table.

Foley performed in a variety of Austin bars early on, but eventually—due to his unreliability, his unflinching and sometimes offensive honesty, his alcoholism, and his generally bizarre behavior—he was banned at all but one, the Austin Outhouse, a bar that became something like a home for him.

Blaze Foley struggled with obesity and the effects of a childhood bout with polio all his life. Some thought his girth indicated jocularity, but that was far from the truth. A passionately honest songwriter, Foley wrote mostly sad songs, songs he could identify with. According to one sound engineer, it was difficult to record Foley's "If I Could Only Fly" because he would "break down in tears" over and over again about halfway through the song.

Foley's other songs touched on political themes, homelessness and, in one case, Girl Scout cookies.

Foley stood out even among the generally weird folks on Austin's music scene. His bizarre behavior made their bizarre behavior look positively average. For one thing, Foley adorned himself with duct tape. It apparently started when he put the gray tape on his boots to parody the metal boot tips in the movie *Urban Cowboy*, but the tape soon found its way all over him. One friend remembers how he used to put duct tape on his jacket in artistic designs. Many took to calling him "The Duct Tape Messiah."

Foley struggled financially all his life. He refused to compromise his art by holding a day job, and he never found wide acceptance outside of the Austin songwriter community.

Though he wrote and recorded a large number of songs, he sold very few. Some masters were lost; some record companies went bankrupt before they could pay him. One legend holds that the FBI or DEA seized the masters for his first album because of its political content, though that has never been verified.

Because of the strange mix of compassion and hard living that defined him, Foley is sometimes also known as "The Gentle Outlaw." One attribute for which Foley is still remembered is that he always stood up for the underprivileged and the weak. In fact, that quality may have cost him his life. He was shot and killed trying to defend a friend named Concho January from his murderous son.

Interest in Blaze Foley and his music has increased since his death in 1989, as evidenced by a documentary that is in the works and by four tribute albums that have appeared. The first three tribute albums consist of well-known artists performing his songs; the fourth is comprised of songs written about him, for him, or otherwise inspired by him.

Blaze Foley was buried in a coffin covered in duct tape. I am not making that up. Townes Van Zandt later remarked that he would have to dig his old friend up to get the pawn shop ticket out of his pocket, so that he could reclaim Blaze's guitar.

A fittingly bizarre end to the life of a true eccentric.

Chapter 47

"The Michelangelo of Armadillo Art"

Jim Franklin
1943-present

Name: Jim Franklin
Lived: 1943-present
Texas connection: Born in Galveston
Occupation: Artist
Claim to weirdness: Psychedelic armadillos, lots of them
Tex-centricity Scale: 9 hipster album covers (out of 10)

After studying art in San Francisco and New York, Jim
Franklin returned to his native Texas and settled in Austin,
where he fell in with the Texas psychedelic movement. He
lived at a "psychedelic music hall" in Austin named the Vulcan
Gas Company and soon found himself drawing posters for
local bands. He started incorporating armadillos into his
posters in 1968, and the armadillo quickly became a symbol of

the hippie movement in Texas.

Franklin became a counterculture phenom. His art adorned the album *Take Me to the Mountains* by Shiva's Headband, which was the first album produced by an Austin act to get a national release. In addition to drawing album covers and posters for bands such as 13th Floor Elevators, Shiva's Headband, and Commander Cody and His Lost Planet Airmen, Franklin also started Armadillo Comics, an underground comic book series.

According to a press release for the "5th Annual Roky Erickson Psychedelic Ice Cream Social celebrating Electro-Shock Survivors," Jim Franklin, the poster artist for the event, is himself an electroshock survivor. In the press release, Franklin said, "I had an elaborate statement prepared in my mind, but in 1965 they erased it with an electric eraser." Jim Franklin joins a group of (some famous, some infamous) Texas eccentrics who also have had the misfortune of receiving shock therapy.

Franklin's art inspired the name for the premiere Austin rock venue of the 1970s, Armadillo World Headquarters. Franklin decorated the site himself with murals and posters. During its heyday, the Armadillo World Headquarters hosted major national rock artists including Frank Zappa, AC/DC, and Dire Straits. At one time it sold more Lone Star beer than any other site in the state except for Houston's Astrodome.

In 1974, Franklin tried his hand at opening his own music venue, The Ritz Theater. It closed after one year.

Today, Franklin does performance art that involves singing and painting on stage. In his free time he builds curved and domed buildings, which he considers another art project. And four decades after he established his fame in one of the weirdest places and weirdest times in Texas history, Jim Franklin—once described as the Michelangelo of Armadillo Art—is still drawing.

Chapter 48

"Texas Medicine"

Clifford Fry, Ph.D.
?-present

Name: Clifford Fry, Ph.D.
Lived: ?-present
Texas connection: Grew up around Kingsville, Texas; based in Houston
Occupation: Economist and musician
Claim to weirdness: Songs like "Her Goodies Aren't as Good as Mine"
Tex-centricity Scale: 4 toe-tappers (out of 10)

Dr. Clifford Fry may well be the only Ph.D. in economics to have made it onto the European Media Service's Top 40 Independent Country chart. He and his eight-piece Houston band have also seen their quirky songs make it onto the World Wide Mainstream Artists Most Played Artist charts and several other European music listings. A little known band making little known songs and landing on little known charts. But hey, they're selling records.

The one word that comes to mind when one listens to a song like "Fat Farm" or "Thoughtful, Helpful Husband" is good clean fun. Okay, that's three words, but you get the idea. The musical style of Dr. Fry's Texas Medicine Band is "old." That's a technical term. It's as if the good doctor went back in time to that singular moment in American musical history right before the term "rock and roll" found currency, when people like Carl Perkins, Jerry Lee Lewis, and Johnny Cash thought they were just playing upbeat country music. It's as if Fry and company bottled that sound, and brought that era back to us. Or, more accurately, brought that sound back to the Europeans, who apparently appreciate Dr. Fry more than his own countrymen.

In a review of the band, Pete Smith of "Pete Smith's Rock Pile" column in *Country Music* says, "Eccentricity in country music means fun blended with good old country music, none of your pop crossover stuff." Based on that definition, Dr. Fry definitely qualifies for eccentric status. In addition to setting innumerable European toes to tapping, Fry's songs have found their way onto PBS's *Car Talk* radio show—has Britney Spears ever done that?—and have been included on several compilations.

A modern-day economist and seven friends making 1950s-era music that is thoroughly enjoyed by Europeans, while little known on this side of the Atlantic—the whole thing is improbable. But it's true.

Chapter 49

"Space in Your Face"

Galactic Cowboys
1989-2000

Names: Monty Colvin, Ben Huggins, Alan Doss, Wally Farkas, and Dane Sonnier
Active: 1989-2000
Texas connection: Based in and around Houston
Occupation: Musicians
Claim to weirdness: They made Texas Christian melodic space metal music
Tex-centricity Scale: 7 flying cow skulls (out of 10)

The Katy, Texas, area is responsible for three bands that have similarities with each other and pretty much no one else on the planet. Galactic Cowboys, King's X, and Atomic Opera are all harmonic heavy metal bands that reached moderate fame in the late 1980s and early 1990s. All three bands are known for cult followings, Christian-influenced and sometimes obscure lyrics, eclectic instruments, melodic harmonies juxtaposed with crunching metal sounds, and a general smiling harmlessness parading in head-banger garb. They are also all connected to Texas music producer Sam Taylor. Strangely, all three bands also have connections to the state of Missouri—in all three cases, band members hail from the Show Me State.

The Galactic Cowboys are by far the zaniest of the three bands. With them, there is yet another street at the rare intersection of art rock, heavy metal, and Christian rock. It's a seldom traveled road known as space rock. There aren't a whole lot of space rock bands out there. Besides the Galactic Cowboys, Pink Floyd, Spacemen 3, and The Flaming Lips are sometimes referred to as space rock bands.

The Galactic Cowboys' album cover art reveals their cosmic interest as well as their sense of humor. The picture on their debut album's cover shows a longhorn cow skull against a black background. Bolts of blue electricity run between the tips of the horns, converging in the precise middle at a symbol of atomic energy. Upon closer inspection, one discovers that the cow skull is in reality a spaceship. The horns are actually wings and the ears are parabolic dishes. The band's second release, 1992's *Space in Your Face*, is illustrated with a photo of a bald man in a space suit. He looks out from the glass globe surrounding his head and reaches his gloved hands toward the camera. The whole scene is bathed in a green glow and in the science fiction-slash-comic book ethos that screams, "This album is not to be taken too seriously."

They don't only sing about space, of course. They also sing about more typical heavy metal themes such as loneliness, anger, and politics; and they sometimes compose lyrics that an average listener might have trouble making make any sense out of. Ranging from ponderous to silly to poetic, the band has put together a body of lyrics that defy easy categorization. They mix the cosmic, the Texan, the light-hearted, the heavy, and the spiritual with a deft touch. Consider these lyrics from their song "Ranch on Mars":

> Someday we'll live among the stars
> Maybe own a ranch on Mars
>
> Come in, come in mission control
> Give us guidance for our souls
> With eyes that scan the universe
> ...
> Our future lies beyond this earth
>
> (©1992, Colvin)

There's the obvious cosmic reference; there's the light-hearted humor of the title and the chorus, and a clear reference to Texana; there's the subtle dark thread of loneliness and not being understood; and there's the spiritual implication. Are we talking about outer space or heaven here?

That's the Galactic Cowboys in a nutshell.

The Galactic Cowboys are also given to flourishes like hidden tracks—if you ever buy the *Space in Your Face* album, fast forward to tracks 21 and 32 after you come to what you think is the end of the CD and you'll find two unadvertised songs. They also like off-the-wall spoken-word fillers between songs. On their debut album, *Galactic Cowboys*, a very irritating principal reads a lunch menu over the school public address system, ending by calling out Friday's fare for the general population, then saying with apparent disgust, "And for our Catholic students...*fish*."

When asked how the band selected their memorable name, lead singer Ben Huggins said, "We thought it was strange, goofy and extremely comic-book-like. It brought together two of the diverse aspects of our home Houston, which is also home to NASA and one of the world's largest rodeos."

In 2000, the Galactic Cowboys released *Let It Go*, which would prove to be their last album. A one-of-a-kind musical experiment had come to an end, but their eccentricity would live on in the form of their albums and mp3 downloads.

Chapter 50

"The Reverend"

Reverend Horton Heat
1959-present

Name: Jim Heath
Lived: 1959-present
Texas connection: Born in Corpus Christi
Occupation: Musician
Claim to weirdness: He makes "country-fed punkabilly" for
the masses
Tex-centricity Scale: 5 hot guitar licks (out of 10)

Jim Heath fell in love with another member of a band he
was in and they got married. (She was a girl.) They both agreed
that the touring lifestyle was not conducive to child-rearing,
and they gave up the music business, theoretically for good.
They soon had a son and a dog named Smokey. (The son's
name wasn't Smokey. Just the dog's.)

Things were hunky-dory, but diapers and formula were expensive. To make extra money, Heath took the old PA system he had used in his former band and started working nights at some local clubs as a sound man.

And then there was treble in paradise. A club owner talked the sound guy into taking the stage during a lull one night, and in response to the boisterous approval of the audience, Jim Heath became the Reverend Horton Heat, a rollicking psychobilly musician prepared to burn up the Dallas music scene.

Mrs. Reverend Horton Heat wasn't happy. She took the child, Smokey the dog, and a variety of Heath's personal effects, and she bolted.

Now, there are a number of ways by which a wronged man can respond in this situation. There's blind fury. There's self-flagellating misery. A momentarily enjoyable descent into a favorite addiction is a possibility. But I'll forever be impressed by the response of Reverend Horton Heat to this unfortunate situation. He penned the lyrics to the song, "Where in the Hell Did You Go with My Toothbrush?"

Lyrics on Horton Heat albums range from the serious, to the funny, to the silly. There are songs about friends with addictions, about Heat's own mother's death, and about cars, girls, and partying. Some songs are pure kitsch, and those songs may be the most popular. "Turkey Gotta Gobble" was borrowed by restaurant chain Boston Market for a Thanksgiving commercial. Other songs have appeared on Mazda ads, Levi's ads, and more. Heat's musical creations have appeared on movie and video game soundtracks.

Among other eccentricities, Heat has the habit of naming his guitar licks. He has one standby that he calls "the hurricane." He has another that's so top secret he won't reveal its name.

As if the outlandish name and the off-kilter songs aren't enough to cement Heat's reputation as one of the most eccentric musicians in Texas, he also has an eye-popping stage presence. He and his band have been called "The Most Electrifying Live Act in America." Considering the fact that they perform approximately 150 live shows per year, they've had plenty of chances to perfect their performance.

As a sometime-actor, Heat has made numerous appearances in the movies and on television shows. But his bread and butter will always be the signature good-times music that has entertained music fans the world over.

Chapter 51

"Electronic, Mechanic, and Social Sound-Sight Interactive Transactional Systems"

Jerry Hunt
1943-1993

Name: Jerry Hunt
Lived: 1943-1993
Texas connection: Born in Waco, died in Canton
Occupation: Composer and "musician"
Claim to weirdness: Ritualistic performances and homemade electronic music devices
Tex-centricity Scale: 10 angelic tablets (out of 10)

I'm not sure it gets any weirder than this.

When hyper-eclectic composer Jerry Hunt recorded his musical creations on paper, he did so using indecipherable phrases such as "a system device of translation gestures [that] provides a string of goals which becomes coherent through reiterative additive uses," "use no start/end mechanism of preparation gesture ensemble," and "select an extent of node content stream elements [using] the same number of sign element increments."

Clear as mud?

Jerry Hunt didn't write music like most composers, using musical notes on a staff, because he didn't compose for normal instruments like pianos, wind instruments, or strings. In fact, the instruments he composed for don't even have names, as they were homemade electronic devices of his own personal design.

Jerry Hunt's music is described in one biography as "a dense micropolyphonic web based on clusters of slow and fast trills....accompanied by a host of high-frequency percussive sounds emphasizing rattles, sleigh bells, wind chimes and the like. Loud and unrelenting, it reminded me of a Texas insect chorus on a hot summer night."

At his performances, Hunt, a bald, bespectacled man in mundane attire, would come out and press a few buttons on his nondescript stack of salvage-yard electronics and the noise—er, music—would start. As this artificial chorus played, apparently random to some extent, Hunt would take out a variety of bizarre props and walk around the stage jumping, pounding them on the floor, or waving them in the air like magic staffs. He would sometimes shout or scream. He has since been compared to a modern day shaman. And that's what we need, isn't it? We need more shamans. (Shamen?)

Hunt's props included broken umbrellas, rattles, homemade bells, and giant phallic symbols. Spectators were uncertain as to whether or not the music was affected by Hunt's movements—sometimes his movements seemed to change the music, and sometimes they didn't. It is now evident that Hunt built his devices with motion sensors, thermometers, and other devices that can interpret human motion or proximity, so that he could at least partially control the musical output via his bizarre ritualistic performances.

Hunt's show was three parts performance art, one part random noise, and one part music, if your definition of music is liberal enough to include such melodic gems as buzzes, spoken voices, whistles, and the sound of "a Radio Shack store during the Holiday shopping season, with all the tacky electronic toys and games sounding off."

Hunt himself called his concerts "…interrelated electronic, mechanic and social sound-sight interactive transactional systems." This seems an adequate description. But so does, "A weird guy on a stage with dangerous electronics hopping around and acting like what he's doing is somehow relevant."

As surprising as all this is, the thing that I find most incredible is that this man was actually able to find an audience in front of which to perform. He also made CDs and videos of his music and, apparently, sold them to human beings from the planet Earth. Album titles include *Ground: Five Mechanic Convention Streams* and *Haramand Plane: Three Translation Links*. Jerry Hunt was a big fan of the colon, apparently. The cover for the *Haramand Plane* album is decorated with modern art. (You expected Norman Rockwell, maybe?)

Hunt was every bit an artist. And by that, I mean he was a total freak show. He collaborated with a "rant" poet named Karen Finley on one project and also worked with a visual artist and other composers. He was on the approval panel for the National Endowment for the Arts in the 1990s, when the first Bush administration famously sought to limit federal funding for controversial artists. Hunt was drawn into the fray because Finley, his collaborator, was one of the artists who had received funding from the NEA.

Now, there are lots of eccentric musicians in Texas. But there isn't one who comes within a million light years of this cat. With Jerry Hunt, the weird just doesn't stop. He is the type of guy who makes the diehard nonconformist crowd smile approvingly and the other 99.99% of the population scratch our heads.

Not only did he make unmusical music using homemade electronic devices—semi-controlled noise, you might call it—and mix this racket with bizarre performance art, but he did so as an expression of his interest in the occult. Yep, it gets weirder. Hard to fathom.

Hunt built the musical language that he programmed into his devices around a set of ancient angelic tablets that a medium named Edward Kelley had given to occultist John Dee in 16th century England. Hunt managed to convert these tablets, which were basically elaborate grids with letters and symbols filling in the squares, into systems for organizing musical notes and playing them back with just the right mix (to him) of order and randomness.

Hunt's occult interests began early. By age 14 he had achieved initiate status into the Rosicrucian Order. Later, while still a teen, he placed ads in various local papers offering instructions on "the path of the infinite" to those who would send in a mail order request to him.

Though Hunt declared himself an atheist in adulthood, his fascination with the occult never wavered. One of his works, "Fluud," is named after a 17th century British mystic, the successor to the aforementioned Dee.

The end of Hunt's story is tragic and no less bizarre than the rest of it. He took his own life after he was diagnosed with terminal lung cancer. Hunt had enjoyed tobacco, both smoked and chewed, for many years. After thoroughly researching methods of suicide, he fashioned a homemade suicide machine that allowed him to breathe enough carbon monoxide to die without putting anyone else at risk. He strapped on a gas mask, twisted a valve, and inhaled his last breath on November 27, 1993.

He left behind perhaps the most unique and inimitable

collection of "music" that the world has ever seen. While he left behind his compositions as well, there is virtually zero chance that another musician will ever come along and cover a Jerry Hunt tune, since no one else can understand what he wrote.

Chapter 52

"Hi, How Are You?"

Daniel Johnston
1961-present

Name: Daniel Dale Johnston
Lived: 1961-present
Texas connection: Lives in Waller, Texas
Occupation: Singer/songwriter and artist
Claim to weirdness: Threw the plane keys out the window.
While flying.
Tex-centricity Scale: 10 frog drawings (out of 10)

The parallels between Daniel Johnston and Roky Erickson are manifold: nurtured by the eclectic Austin music community; heralded as geniuses by well-known musical acts; the subjects of documentaries; still performing after many years.

Born in California and raised in West Virginia, Johnston

first came to Texas to attend Abilene Christian University. He later moved to Houston to live with his brother. While there, Johnston began recording songs in the basement on a boom box. After relocating to Austin, he started handing out cassettes of his music to friends. In time, Johnston developed a cult following in the capital city—Austinites like to be members of "cult followings"—and record stores started selling his tapes. A small record label eventually released Johnston's tunes to the Austin record-buying public; soon thereafter Johnston was featured on an MTV special about Austin.

After the "Cutting Edge" program aired on MTV, Johnston became a minor celebrity. His albums began to sell outside the boundaries of the Lone Star State. During the time of his growing popularity, Johnston was asked to paint the smiling frog Jeremiah from the cover of his first album, *Hi, How Are You?* on the side of a building in Austin. As time went by, the mural became a piece of folk art; it was vehemently defended when a buyer of the building considered removing it in 2004.

Johnston's Beatles-inspired music focused on his fundamentalist Christian beliefs, comic books, television characters, and his unrequited love for a lady named Laurie. Johnston's lyrics often reflect a strange mix of childishness and brooding.

After playing at Austin's renowned South by Southwest music show (known by the abbreviation SXSW) in 1991, Johnston had a breakdown while flying back to West Virginia in his father's small airplane. Johnston the younger wrestled the keys from the plane's ignition and threw them out of a window. Johnston's father, a World War II pilot, managed to crash land the airplane, which was destroyed. Both men walked away from the crash uninjured. Daniel Johnston was confined to a hospital after this incident; during his time in the hospital, he aired his songs on a radio show.

Johnston's transformation from hospital inpatient to touring musician has been, in the words of The Grateful Dead, a long, strange trip. Much of Johnston's national notoriety stems from the fact that several musicians have themselves been fans of his strange work. Nirvana lead singer Kurt Cobain often referenced Daniel Johnston in interviews and sported a shirt emblazoned with the artwork from his first album at the 1992 MTV Music Awards.

But Cobain wasn't the only rocker to appreciate Johnston's oddball artistry: artists from The Butthole Surfers to Eddie Vedder to Sonic Youth have been linked to him and his music. Beck and Tom Waits, among others, have covered Daniel Johnston tunes. Sometimes artists like to "be different," and covering a Daniel Johnston tune makes you pretty different—odds are, you won't see Mariah Carey singing "Casper the Friendly Ghost" anytime soon.

Johnston's music and life have been featured in a number of theater productions, including "Love Defined" at New York's Joyce Theater and a rock opera called "Speeding Motorcycle" produced by a Texas production company in 2005. Also in 2005, a Dutch documentary about his life was released, as was *The Devil and Daniel Johnston*, a Director's Award winner at the Sundance Film Festival, now available from Sony Home Entertainment.

Johnston's music career has flourished. He signed a deal with one major label (Atlantic), and was on the verge of signing with another (Elektra), a deal he rejected.

Johnston's website lists no fewer than 26 Daniel Johnston albums recorded since 1980, including his own label (Eternal Yip Eye Music). His touring schedule has been relatively busy, too, with 55 tour dates in 2007 and 2008, tours that saw him perform in dozens of cities throughout North America and Europe. In addition, Johnston's cartoonish art has been exhibited in museums from Burbank to Paris to Copenhagen.

Johnston's life has taken several twists and turns since, as a child, he "used to bang around on the piano" and make up songs while he mowed the lawn. It has taken him through dark valleys of illness and onto sun-drenched peaks of creative genius. Despite his struggles, Johnston has spent his life creating music that has influenced some of the most popular musicians in the world.

Chapter 53

"She Dared to Be Different"

Janis Joplin
1943-1970

Name: Janis Lyn Joplin
Lived: 1943-1970
Texas connection: Born and raised in Port Arthur
Occupation: *Rolling Stone*'s 46th Greatest Artist of All Time
Claim to weirdness: Flamboyant clothes and a very liberated lifestyle
Tex-centricity Scale: 8 bottles of Southern Comfort (out of 10)

Janis Joplin grew up tormented by classmates in Port Arthur. She had been a bright and artistic little girl but junior high brought acne, a few extra pounds, and the derisive jeers of the other kids. Joplin was rejected not only because of her appearance but also because, in her words, "I was a misfit. I read. I painted."

Joplin responded to her social rejection by rejecting society. She accumulated a vast repertoire of profanities, an outlandish wardrobe and a proclivity for sexual and chemical exploits—the main chemical at that time in her life being alcohol, most notably Southern Comfort whiskey, which led to her being even further isolated. The free spirit found few friends in the very conservative community of Port Arthur where even her own mother was a Sunday school teacher.

She finally fell in with a group of beatniks at her high school and found happiness trolling night spots in southeast Texas and Louisiana. During this time in her life she was first exposed to the black jazz music that would inspire and later define her.

Joplin first went to college in Beaumont but found no acceptance there, either, remaining an outcast. She transferred to the University of Texas at Austin and began playing her music at Threadgill's, a still-famous-today local hangout that was then owned by a country music fan and one-time bootlegger, Kenneth Threadgill. Threadgill would become Joplin's lifelong friend.

She also found acceptance at a counterculture haven known as The Ghetto, where she spent most of her time. Her social problems persisted among some parts of the student body, however. For example, she was nominated by one fraternity for the annual "Ugliest Man on Campus" contest. The campus newspaper was a bit more diplomatic. When it ran an article about the unapologetic hippie, the title was "She Dares to Be Different."

Joplin, a less-than-stellar student, eventually moved to the San Francisco area looking for acceptance among the considerable nonconformist population of the Bay Area. She spent two years playing music, dressing strangely, and making weird friends. She also started using drugs like heroin and methamphetamine. Eventually, her profuse drug use left her emaciated; concerned friends threw a "bus fare party" to raise money so she could go home to her parents and get help.

Life back in Port Arthur was completely different. Joplin adopted a more traditional lifestyle and wardrobe, even wearing a beehive hairdo for a time, and stayed drug free. This restrained lifestyle would not last, however. In 1966, Joplin responded to an invitation to join a psychedelic band called Big Brother and the Holding Company, based in Haight-Ashbury, near San Francisco.

Joplin's meteoric rise began in August 1967 when she performed with her band at the Monterey Pop Festival alongside Jimi Hendrix and others. Stardom would follow the many positive reviews of her band's performance there. Joplin herself earned acclaim for her soulful, searing vocals. Magazines as weighty as *Time* and *Vogue* respectively heralded her arrival, calling her "the most powerful singer to emerge from the white rock movement," and "the most staggering leading woman in rock."

The next three years would see a dizzying flurry of activity for Joplin. She toured and recorded first with Big Brother and the Holding Company and then with the Kozmic Blues Band, performing with the latter at Woodstock in 1969. (She would form the Full Tilt Boogie band in 1970.) She also became well-known for speaking her mind about the plentiful social ills of the country and was a frequent guest on television programs, including repeat appearances on *The Dick Cavett Show.*

As her career took off, her eccentric ways did anything but diminish. She was known for her bright, psychedelic outfits, feathers in her hair, beads, body art, political and social outspokenness, and an eager willingness to communicate with four-letter words.

She also became notorious for a string of love affairs with individuals from both sides of the gender aisle, and for her voracious appetite for illegal substances. A lover of hers at that time, Peggy Caserta, said that Joplin was injecting $200 worth of heroin every day.

Joplin then moved to Brazil. Away from the users who had become her friends, she was able to kick drugs for awhile. However, when she came back to the U.S. her heroin abuse and destructive friendships resumed full tilt. On October 4, 1970, while working on the studio album that would become her best-selling recording of all time (*Pearl*), Joplin died of a heroin overdose in her hotel room. She was 27 years old at the time of her death.

During her short life, Janis Joplin did indeed dare to be different. And being different made her great, but it also made her suffering great. The very eccentricity that enabled her to sing the way she wanted may have driven her to her death.

Chapter 54

"Three Kings"

King's X
1980-present

Names: Doug Pinnick, Ty Tabor, and Jerry Gaskill
Active: 1980-present
Texas connection: Based in Katy, Texas
Occupation: VH1's 83rd Greatest Artist of Hard Rock
Claim to weirdness: Heavy metal with sitars and C.S. Lewis-inspired lyrics
Tex-centricity Scale: 7 obscure lyrics (out of 10)

King's X, like fellow oddball head-bangers the Galactic Cowboys, came to semi-prominence in the late 1980s while performing in the Houston area from their base in Katy, Texas. Like the Cowboys, King's X was nominally labeled a heavy metal band, but they were unlike any heavy metal band in existence then (or ever, really). Yes, they had loud electric guitars and speaker-rattling drumbeats, but they also had Beatles-inspired harmonies, lyrics straight out of C.S. Lewis' world of Christian fantasy, and instruments such as sitars, more commonly found in India than in your average heavy metal venue. Also odd for heavy metal, King's X had a black lead singer. Besides Jimi Hendrix and 1980's flash-in-the-pan Living Colour, very few metal acts of note have crossed the color barrier.

The three men who made up King's X first came together in Springfield, Missouri, as a touring band for contemporary Christian recording artist Phil Keaggy. Soon, they launched their own band on the side and played top forty hits on the bar and club circuit around Springfield. The band went through a couple of very 80's-sounding names (Sneak Preview, The Edge) before moving to Houston, Texas, and letting ZZ Top video producer Sam Taylor rename them King's X.

From the start, King's X eschewed the label of "Christian band." While the lyrics on their first three albums were clearly inspired by the Bible and by concepts found in the writings of Christian fantasy author C.S. Lewis—their first album, in fact, was named after Lewis' Christian science fiction novel *Out of the Silent Planet*—they never recorded on a Christian music label, and they wrote and performed music that was way too heavy for airtime on contemporary Christian radio stations.

Many Christian music stores didn't carry their albums, unsure of what to do with a heavy metal trio recording for the same Megaforce Records that gave the world Anthrax, Metallica, and the distinctively un-Christian band Ministry.

Their sound was unlike anything the Christian world (or the heavy metal world, for that matter) had ever heard, with its haunting harmonies and its dreamy, poetic lyrics. Many attempts have been made in trying to describe the King's X sound over the years. One writer described it as "the kind of music you might expect if C. S. Lewis, the Beatles, Jimi Hendrix, and AC/DC were thrown into a blender." (I imagine a different kind of music if you threw those guys into a blender, actually. A squishy kind of music.)

Unfortunately for King's X, listeners were equally unsure of what to do with them. While mainstream hard rock acts of 1989 were releasing popular, simple-minded songs like Aerosmith's "Love in an Elevator" and Motley Crue's "Dr. Feelgood," King's X came out with "Pleiades," a song with the lyrics, "Who can restrain Pleiades/Or know the laws of heavenlies?/How many times have we been wrong before?"

Deep. Maybe too deep. This was heavy metal for the thinking man of faith. The problem was, most record-buying headbangers were apparently little interested in spirituality or artistry, and most Christian music fans weren't particularly interested in banging their heads. Turns out, as King's X and the Galactic Cowboys can both almost certainly confirm, the Christian heavy metal fan base is relatively small.

The song "Pleiades" appeared on what is now regarded by many fans as the best King's X album of all, *Gretchen Goes to Nebraska*, which came packaged with a somewhat rambling short story about a girl, Gretchen, who, well, goes to Nebraska. (You'd have to read it.)

This album, their second, established a core following for the band that would last through the release of 12 more albums as of this writing. Even today, King's X maintains a fiercely loyal fan base that has made it possible for them to survive almost twenty years.

King's X has been heralded by many well-known musicians as a major influence and a major part of rock history. One artist, Pearl Jam bassist Jeff Ament, credited the band with the invention of grunge music. The band itself was recognized by VH1 as one of the top 100 Artists of Hard Rock, and the individual members have been repeatedly recognized for their contributions to the development of rock and roll. Mark Joseph, in his "On the Dark Side" article for Christian zine *re:generation quarterly* noted, "On any serious rock and roll connoisseur's list of the top ten bands of all time, you're sure to find King's X. They're not as well known as the Beatles and the Stones—their album sales generally top out around 200,000. But if you don't believe their fans, just ask the bands that have asked the Houston trio to open for them—Pearl Jam, AC/DC, Aerosmith, Metallica, the Scorpions, and others."

The King's X sound evolved as their career went forward. They followed *Gretchen Goes to Nebraska* with their best-selling album, *Faith, Hope, Love*, a disc which reached number 85 on the U.S. charts. After the success of this album, the band signed with a major label, Atlantic, for whom they would produce three albums of original material. Each album was successively harder and more muscular than the one before, and the spiritual and poetic lyrics of their earliest albums were replaced by words that ranged from brooding and angry to incomprehensible. The band was dropped after three records due to poor sales and returned to independent labels for the release of their next seven collections.

Complicating the problem King's X had in connecting with a wide audience was a tendency by the members of the band to record songs with lyrics that made absolutely no sense whatsoever. Take, for example, the song "Six Broken Soldiers" from the *Faith, Hope, Love* album, the lyrics of which include:

> i dont care if youre sick what can i possibly do with an american library and a contract on you ive got six broken soldiers in the trunk of my car two of them speak four go to bars rods in the closet a six shooter in hand a caged up gorilla and three local bands...
>
> (©1990 jetydosa music/ackee music)

Huh?

Very little could take a band like King's X and make it any more bizarre than it already was. But this happened in 1998 when lead singer Doug Pinnick (he has since changed his first name to Dug) revealed in a magazine interview that he was gay.

Now, if it was hard to sell records as a Christian heavy metal band with a penchant for poetic lyrics and airy Oriental instruments on an independent secular label, and if it was hard to sell records as a nominally-Christian metal band with a penchant for angry and hard-to-interpret lyrics that sometimes included expressions like, "I guess I lost my faith" on a major label—well, it would be even more difficult to sell records as such a band with an openly gay lead singer. After Pinnick's announcement, King's X was dropped by their Christian music distributer. Their core following remained faithful, however, and they continued to produce and sell records.

Folks, it just doesn't get much weirder than King's X on the music scene. One thing you can say for them, though, is that they are definitely their own band. In the end, they decided to make the music they liked. And music fans who share an interest in Christianity, Beatles-esque harmonies, Indian string instruments, science fiction and fantasy, Jimi Hendrix-style vocals and ambiguous lyrics, will simply love this band. (Yeah, it's a niche market.)

Chapter 55

"The Thinking Man's Cowboy"

Lyle Lovett
1957-present

Name: Lyle Pearce Lovett
Lived: 1957-present
Texas connection: Born in Klein, Texas
Occupation: Hard-to-classify country singer and bouffant-haired actor
Claim to weirdness: The pompadour, definitely
Tex-centricity Scale: 7 songs about fat girls (out of 10)

Lyle Lovett's first album, released in 1986, included five Top Forty country singles. Since then, many have considered him a country singer. That, my friends, is a gross oversimplification. From the beginning, Lovett has combined diverse influences such as jazz, blues, folk, country, swing, bluegrass, pop, and gospel to create his own eclectic sound.

In recent years, Lovett's sound has been lumped in with other hard-to-categorize artists under the "alternative country" umbrella. In addition to the range of musical styles, he has set himself apart from mainstream country acts with his witty, insightful lyrics and his odd look—his piled-up pompadour alone has helped transform him into a nationally-recognizable personality. Some of the better-known of his zany songs include "The Fat Girl," "Don't Touch My Hat," and "Fiona," a ditty about a six-foot-tall, one-eyed lady from the bayou whose prettier sister "just won't do."

The New Yorker magazine has labeled Lyle Lovett "The Thinking Man's Cowboy." The fact that Lyle Lovett is even mentioned in *The New Yorker* should illustrate that he is not your typical country artist. While *The New Yorker* praises Lovett's "sophisticated song crafting" and his "tightly constructed" concerts, a quick search of the archives reveals no mention whatsoever of several more traditional country artists.

An actor as well as a critically-acclaimed musician, Lovett has had upwards of thirty roles in movies and television shows, oftentimes portraying a country singer, but also playing characters as diverse as a research scientist and a disc jockey.

It was in his role as Detective DeLongpre in 1992's *The Player* that Lovett first met actress Julia Roberts. They fell in love and were married after a three-week whirlwind romance.

This relationship thrust Lovett in front of the glare of the international entertainment media in a way that his music and his pompadour hadn't.

Lovett and Roberts were often portrayed as an odd couple in the media. Their relationship dissolved after 21 months, though they remain close friends to this day.

This unconventional small-town Texan who once played guitar on his front porch with fellow Texas A&M Aggie Robert Earl Keen has crafted himself into a widely-acclaimed musician with the down-home appeal of a simple man. This approach has set him apart from the polished mainstream of popular country music, but it has also resulted in a loyal following and the respect of artistic communities from Austin to New York City.

But the hair. I mean, come on.

Chapter 56

"The Weirdness"

MC 900 Ft. Jesus
c. 1957-present

Name: Mark Griffin
Lived: c. 1957-present
Texas connection: Lives in Dallas
Occupation: Former musician
Claim to weirdness: The stage name, the music, and the disappearing act
Tex-centricity Scale: 7 spoken word songs (out of 10)

Mark Griffin, aka MC 900 Ft. Jesus, released one EP and three albums between 1990 and 1994 and then vanished from the music scene and got a pilot's license. The albums he released were notable for their unique blend of rap, spoken word, jazz, and unadulterated weirdness.

Some of his songs have a very mainstream rap sound and

stand apart from typical hip hop only because of their intelligent and often amusing lyrics. However, MC 900 Ft. Jesus was an artsy rapper, if such a thing is possible. In the words of musicianguide.com, Griffin created "a quirky sound that blends rap rhythms with socially conscious lyrics and bits of classic jazz."

As an artist, Mr. Jesus made several off-the-wall, avant-garde tunes. One ditty, "Dali's Handgun," takes lines from a variety of surrealist poems and clabbers them together to make a statement about firearms.

Yeah, he's that weird.

Another song, "Born with Monkey Asses," sounds a lot like an angry parent shouting at a school board meeting but is, in reality, a paranoid schizophrenic patient's profane rant about what he thinks doctors do with research animals at night.

In another song, "Tiptoe through the Inferno," Griffin's droning, hesitating voice says nonsensical unrhymed verses like, "Do not make the mistake of believing that I am the person who is speaking to you now," and, "Please do not obfuscate matters with science or other baloney…sandwiches," and, "Please, do not change color while I am talking to you." These gems are layered on top of the strains of impromptu jazz.

Griffin was an army brat. Born in Kentucky, he went to high school in Germany, Belgium, and Virginia. He studied music at Morehead State University and, at the graduate level, at North Texas State University (now UNT) in Denton.

Griffin's music often deals with the mentally ill and, perhaps similarly, the super-religious. The bizarre stage name MC 900 Ft. Jesus is a pot shot at both the rap industry and the religion industry. On the one hand, Griffin chose the name because he wanted a ridiculously long and hard-to-remember MC name to parody the invented names of popular rap artists. He found his ridiculously long name when he read about a vision televangelist Oral Roberts had in which a 900 foot Jesus Christ appeared to him and reassured him that he would not go broke. (Few people realize that Jesus was not only Oral Roberts' Savior but also his financial advisor.)

Quite possibly the strangest part of the MC 900 Ft. Jesus story is his disappearance from the music scene. After *One Step Ahead of the Spider* came out in 1994, Mr. Jesus all but vanished. He made a minor splash when Spike Jonze made a video for the song "If I Only Had a Brain" from that album, but he hasn't been heard from since. Internet chat rooms are rife with pleas from music fans—particularly fans of jazz and dance music—for the second coming of MC 900 Ft. Jesus. In response to one plea, the very private Griffin granted an interview with earpollution.com and explained that he still has one record left on the deal with his label, but that neither he nor his label are in much of a hurry to make it. Meanwhile, he has been playing trumpet on the North Texas music scene and sometimes works as a DJ at a dance club.

The weirdness of Mark Griffin hasn't died. It's just gone low-key.

Chapter 57

"Bat Out of Hell"

Meat Loaf
1947-present

Name: Marvin Lee Aday (later legally changed to Michael Lee Aday)
Lived: 1947-present
Texas connection: Born in Dallas
Occupation: Rock musician
Claim to weirdness: The stage name, for one
Tex-centricity Scale: 6 bankruptcies (out of 10)

Meat Loaf got his nickname when, as a teen, he took a dare and let a Volkswagen run over his head. A witness told him afterward that he must have meatloaf for brains, and the name stuck. Meat Loaf's music career began after his mother had died and he left his abusive father behind in Dallas. His first band was Meat Loaf Soul, and their first gig had them opening for Van Morrison's band in Huntington Beach, California. Soon, Meat Loaf was participating in theater, acting in the Broadway version of *Hair* and in a production called *More Than You Deserve.*

In 1973, Mr. Loaf was asked to appear in *The Rocky Horror Picture Show* play and, later, in the movie of the same name. Meanwhile, his singing career was poised to take off. A video of a Meat Loaf song appeared as a trailer attached to *The Rocky Horror Picture Show* and he provided vocals on an album by rocker Ted Nugent.

In 1977, Loaf released his seminal album *Bat Out of Hell,* the product of a tumultuous creative relationship with songwriter Jim Steinman, with whom Mr. Loaf would trade a number of lawsuits over the years. They would eventually settle their differences and collaborate on future albums, including *Bat Out of Hell II and Bat Out of Hell III.*

Meat Loaf's success seemed assured. He appeared on *Saturday Night Live* and sold out a number of venues after the release of the first *Bat Out of Hell* album. But it would not be that easy. Mr. Loaf inexplicably lost his voice while recording his second album and soon found himself battling drug addiction. During the ensuing years, Loaf would file for bankruptcy more than once.

The 1980s saw Meat Loaf's voice come back and also saw him release a number of less successful albums. This despite the fact that *Bat Out of Hell* remained on the UK Top 200 chart throughout the 1980s and, indeed, has never left that chart.

Fortune smiled on Mr. Loaf, however, in the 1990s. In 1992, he released *Bat Out of Hell II* to critical acclaim. A single from that album, "I'd Do Anything for Love (But I Won't Do That)," reached number one in over two dozen countries and helped to earn him a Grammy award. Other successful albums have followed, as have film roles in movies as divergent as *Tenacious D in: The Pick of Destiny, Leap of Faith,* and *Fight Club.* Meanwhile, his touring schedule has

219

featured hundreds of sold-out shows around the world.

The rock and roll lifestyle hasn't been easy on Meat Loaf. He has suffered from acute laryngitis, multiple concussions (possibly as a result of the Volkswagen episode, or, if not that, then maybe as a result of the time a shot put was dropped on his head—I'm not making this stuff up), and a serious heart condition known as Wolff-Parkinson-White syndrome, a disease so important it gets three names. Also well-documented is Loaf's ongoing battle with obesity.

Meat Loaf, once a little boy named Marvin from Dallas— the son of a school teacher and an alcoholic father—has become a worldwide phenomenon, a rock and roll cult hero of massive proportions (figuratively and literally), and an instantly recognizable face on the television or movie screen.

It takes a big man to present himself to the public under the name Meat Loaf, but Marvin Lee Aday has done just that. With dozens of television and movie appearances, and with no fewer than six platinum albums in the US and the UK, Meat Loaf has made a name for himself, a name unlike any other.

Chapter 58

"King of the Road"

Roger Miller
1936-1992

Name: Roger Dean Miller
Lived: 1936-1992
Texas connection: Born in Fort Worth
Occupation: Musician and television personality
Claim to weirdness: Nine words: "My Uncle Used to Love Me but She Died"
Tex-centricity Scale: 6 nonsense syllables (out of 10)

"Make you wanna say hidey-ho!
Burns your tummy, don'tcha know.
Chug-a-lug, chug-a-lug."
So sang Roger Miller in his song "Chug-a-Lug," a catchy tune that illustrates Miller's witty and often light-hearted songwriting style. He balanced a catalogue of fun songs like

this with more serious songs, including the monster 1964 hit "King of the Road."

Miller found great success in the early 1960s with his brand of good-natured music, nominally classified as country even though it really didn't sound much like the country music of that time. He was so popular, in fact, that in 1964 and 1965 he won 11 Grammy awards.

Miller was born in Fort Worth. He moved to Oklahoma to live with an uncle after his father died. In quotes attributed to him on his website, Miller looks back at his difficult childhood in Oklahoma through the ever-present lens of humor, noting that he even "flunked school bus." He added:

> The school I went to had 37 students, me and 36 Indians. One time we had a school dance and it rained for 36 days straight. During recess we used to play cowboy and Indians and things got pretty wild from my standpoint.

Miller was influenced by a native of his hometown in Oklahoma, Sheb Wooley, who married Miller's cousin. Wooley became a musician and actor, noted for his novelty song "The Purple People Eater." He taught Miller his first guitar chords. When Roger Miller was a teen, he was desperate to own a guitar. He stole one, but he turned himself in the next day and, to avoid jail time, he joined the army. (Miller has since joked that he got his education in Korea, "Clash of '52.")

After his stint in the military, Miller moved to Nashville. He worked as a singing bellhop and eventually landed a job as fiddle-player for Minnie Pearl. Soon, Roger Miller was writing songs for the likes of George Jones and even put out his own single, which went nowhere.

After the birth of his son Alan, Miller decided to quit the music business and took a job as a firefighter in Amarillo. Unable to shake the music bug, he fought fires during the day and played clubs at night. After he slept through a fire, he was encouraged to get out of the firefighting business.

Miller was "rediscovered" by Ray Price in Amarillo and offered a job with his touring group. He wrote the hit song "Invitation to the Blues" for Price shortly thereafter. This song rose to number three on the country charts and cemented Miller's reputation as a songwriter. A publishing deal with a record company followed, and that deal produced a string of hits, including Jim Reeves' number one hit "Billy Bayou." In the years that followed, Miller kept writing songs and also tried his hand at recording.

Miller found little success as a solo artist and saw his marriage fall apart under the strain of his music career and his "wild child" reputation. During this time he wasn't making as much money as he needed to live, and things would only get worse when he was dropped by RCA.

But things would turn around quickly. Smash Records was an upstart that was producing upbeat pop numbers like "Hey! Baby" (produced by fellow Texas eccentric Major Bill Smith) and "My Boyfriend's Back." After a chance meeting with the principals of this company at a bar, Miller was offered $1600 for 16 songs. He started recording a couple of months later, bringing 12 of his own songs with him. Those songs included "Dang Me" and "Chug-a-Lug," signature songs that captured Miller's unique style. Many songs with similar silly themes, nonsense syllables, and catchy tunes would follow.

Miller took his earnings and moved to California. After "Dang Me" hit the Top Forty radio waves, Miller's career took off. The infectious song stood up to the British invasion and shot to the top of the pop charts. Because everyone in Nashville knew Roger Miller, it flew up the country charts as well. Miller began to tour relentlessly. Because of his propensity to deliver witty one-liners, he became a favorite of entertainment journalists and was featured in all the major magazines.

Miller's next hit was "Chug-a-Lug." Although a bit

controversial among the traditional country fan base due to its subject, it was a raging success anyway. This was followed by "Do Wacka Do," which was only a minor hit, but Miller's greatest moment was in the offing.

While travelling outside Chicago, he saw a sign that said "Trailers for sale or rent," and spent the next six weeks penning "King of the Road." The rest is history. "King of the Road" was the biggest hit of his career and was the reason that, after winning an improbable five Grammies in 1964, he was able to follow with an even more incredible six Grammies in 1965.

Miller landed his own short-lived television variety show, but it only lasted three episodes, despite Miller's effortless use of folksy humor. His recording and songwriting career slowed after the television show, and Smash Records eventually folded. Though he continued to tour and eventually signed with Columbia Records, the number one hits stopped coming.

A new phase in his career began in 1985, when *Big River*, a Broadway play about Huck Finn, featured a score by Miller. The musical was a smash, and Miller won a Tony Award for best score, making Roger Miller the only country music artist ever to win a Tony.

After Miller died of lung cancer in 1992, he was inducted into the Country Music Hall of Fame. Numerous other honors have followed, including being ranked by CMT as 23rd on the list of the 40 Greatest Men in Country Music.

Roger Miller is a one-of-a-kind character in American music history, too unique for country or pop music to contain him, too funny and accessible not to catch the attention of the American record-buying public. In the words of the tribute to him published on the Roger Miller website, he was "equal parts laughter and soul."

Chapter 59
"The Cult Movie Icon"

Jack Nance
1943-1996

Name: Marvin John Nance
Lived: 1943-1996
Texas connection: Raised in Dallas
Occupation: Actor
Claim to weirdness: Quirky characters and mysterious death
Tex-centricity Scale: 9 weird movies (out of 10)

Jack Nance, the son of a Neiman Marcus CEO, toured the country doing children's theater before settling in at the American Conservatory Theater in San Francisco for eight years. While there, he got involved in avant-garde theater and soon hooked up with oddball movie-maker David Lynch, who was working on a student film production called *Eraserhead*. The bizarre movie about a man and a deformed, otherworldly infant was ridiculed by the press but embraced by underground movie fans, and it launched both Nance and Lynch into cult stardom.

Following this performance, Nance would be cast in every Lynch production except for one. His most noteworthy role was that of Pete Martell in the decidedly weird Lynch TV series *Twin Peaks*. He acted in a number of non-Lynch productions as well, but he was almost always associated with quirky, non-mainstream work.

This cult movie icon appeared in dozens of films, but in most of them his time on screen amounted to little more than a few seconds. He could have certainly appeared in more films if not for his problems with motivation and alcoholism. At one point, Nance left Los Angeles "for good," and returned to his hometown of Dallas. Lynch tracked him down, however, and convinced him to appear in another movie.

It was on the set of this movie, *Blue Velvet*, that Nance befriended costar Dennis Hopper, a man who had battled alcoholism and won. Nance begged Hopper for help, and Hopper helped Nance get into rehab.

During his time in rehab, Nance met Kelly Jean van Dyke, the daughter of *Coach* co-star Jerry van Dyke. The two were married in 1991. Van Dyke was Nance's second wife.

When Kelly Jean slipped back into drug abuse and started working in the porn industry to make money, Nance fought to save her. In the end, while he was in Yosemite National Park shooting *Meatballs 4*, he called her and told her that if she didn't get clean he would have to leave. He couldn't continue to be around the drinking and the drugs, he told her, without falling back into the trap of alcoholism. They argued. She told him that if he hung up the phone, she would kill herself. There was a storm raging outside in Yosemite and suddenly, the phone line went dead.

The camp phones were dead. Nance and a friend raced to the nearest police station. The cops there called the LAPD and had an officer sent to check on Kelly Jean. The call came back a few minutes later; she had hanged herself.

Two years after Kelly Jean's death, Nance decided to start drinking again. The rest of his life was a blur of drunkenness, small parts in B movies, and disappointment. On a December day in 1996, Nance had lunch with two friends. The friends noticed that Nance had a bruise under one eye and asked him about it. The actor claimed that he had been walking across a donut shop parking lot and mouthed off to a couple of Hispanic men about their dress, telling them to get a job. One of the young men socked him in the eye and knocked him down, he said.

The next day, one of the friends Nance had had lunch with went to check on him. He was dead from internal head injuries. The police initially ruled his death a homicide, though much doubt remains about whether the attack actually happened, or whether Nance simply got drunk and fell down and used the story to cover the fact that he was falling-down drunk early in the morning.

A strange life. A strange death. Jack Nance's story is a tragic tale of Texas eccentricity.

Chapter 60

"Red Headed Stranger"

Willie Nelson
1933-present

Name: Willie Hugh Nelson
Lived: 1933-present
Texas connection: Born and raised in Abbott, Texas
Occupation: Musician
Claim to weirdness: Bio-Willie
Tex-centricity Scale: 5 doobies (out of 10)

Willie Nelson is a Texas icon and a pioneer of outlaw country music. He is widely known for his efforts not only on behalf of farmers (he helped establish Farm Aid, a 1985 concert benefiting America's farmers), but also as an advocate for U.S. troops. Besides being philanthropic, Willie is also known for his enjoyment of an occasional cannabis cigarette. In a 2008 biography, Nelson was reported to have smoked his first joint at 10 years of age, and was said to have lit up in the White House when he was a guest of President Jimmy Carter.

Nelson is also remembered for once owing over $16 million in back taxes to the IRS, which he paid by auctioning off many of his possessions and by putting out an album called *The IRS Tapes: Who'll Buy My Memories?*

Always an atypical country music star—an anti-star, if you will— Nelson has been associated with an impressive and odd assortment of musicians, including Julio Iglesias, Kris Kristofferson, Sinead O'Connor, Johnny Cash, Kid Rock, Waylon Jennings, The Beach Boys, Merle Haggard, David Crosby, Bonnie Raitt, Paul Simon, Bob Dylan, and Phish, among others.

Nelson's real start in the music business came in Nashville, where he won a publishing contract and wrote a number of songs, including Patsy Cline's blockbuster "Crazy." After his Nashville career faltered, he relocated to Austin and became a local superstar. His 1975 album *Red Headed Stranger* was a mega-hit, and Nelson never looked back. Dozens of movie and television roles followed, as did several number one hits, including "Always on my Mind" and "On the Road Again."

Nelson has also been associated with a number of political activities, most of them left-of-center. He has advocated for the legalization of marijuana, has raised money for tsunami victims, has pushed for an end to horse slaughtering, and has campaigned for liberal politicians like Presidential candidate Dennis Kucinich and fellow Texas eccentric Kinky Friedman. Any doubts about his liberal credentials were erased in 2007 when ice cream mega-corporation Ben & Jerry's named a flavor after him, "Willie Nelson's Country Peach Cobbler Ice Cream."

Nelson has recently risen to prominence for his activities in promoting Bio-Willie, a brand of biodiesel sold at two filling stations (one in Texas and one in Oregon). Biodiesel is a fuel that can burn in diesel engines but is made of renewable vegetable oils.

During his career, Nelson has won multiple Grammy, CMA, CMT, and Music City News awards for his work. He has been married five times and has fathered ten children. Meanwhile, he has somehow managed to remain relevant through four decades, ever since signing his first record deal in 1961. The Red Headed Stranger is a stranger no more. The pot-smoking, progressive-leaning country music outlaw is heralded worldwide.

His braids, bandana, instantly recognizable voice and guitar are known the world over and he has made a career for himself by being brilliantly Willie.

Chapter 61

"A Child's Odyssey"

Kermit Oliver
1943-present

Name: Kermit Oliver
Lived: 1933-present
Texas connection: Born in Refugio, Texas; lives in Waco
Occupation: Artist
Claim to weirdness: Surreal art
Tex-centricity Scale: 4 fancy French scarves (out of 10)

One of the really weird things about Kermit Oliver is that, though his paintings sell for five figures, and though he is the first American artist to have designed scarves for the renowned fashion house Hermés in Paris, and though he is known to art collectors the world over, and though his works can be found in permanent collections in respected museums like Houston's Museum of Fine Arts and the Art Museum of Southeast

Texas—despite all this, he works as a mail sorter for the U.S. Postal Service and lives a secluded life in Waco, Texas.

The other weird thing about him is the work itself: Oliver's paintings are known for their realism, their basis in Old and New Testament and Greek and Roman mythologies, and their simultaneous depiction of rural Texas themes. Oliver's works combine the traditionally Texan with the decidedly classical in a style he himself has named "symbolic realism."

Oliver, the son of a working Refugio cowboy, has lived an unexpected life. An African-American from rural Texas, he has made a name for himself in the international art world, all while remaining in Waco.

Though he never moved to Paris or New York, his high-end silk scarves have been profiled in trendy rags like *Vogue* magazine. His paintings and woodcuts and sketches have been displayed around the world. And his distinctive style, one that takes contemporary ideas and presents them in a classical style, but with the bizarre intrusions of surrealistic oddities, has set him apart from other contemporary American artists.

The body of Oliver's work shows the deep imprint that was left on his heart as he made his odyssey through a rural upbringing on the ranches of South Texas. Even though he didn't follow in his father's footsteps to become a ranch hand, the cowboy life was never far away from him. Farm animals and working cowboys figure in his narrative paintings, as do landscapes that are distinctively Texan.

Kermit Oliver is a one-of-a-kind artist, one who eschewed fame and embraced small-town life, and one who has produced a lifetime of inimitable art that inspires collectors around the globe, all while sorting mail during the day.

Chapter 62

"The Singing Cowboy"

Red River Dave
1914-2002

Name: Dave McEnery
Lived: 1914-2002
Texas connection: Born in San Antonio
Occupation: Musician and entertainer
Claim to weirdness: Songs about Exxon, the Falklands War, and Barney Clark
Tex-centricity Scale: 6 B movies (out of 10)

Red River Dave, it was noted in his obituary in the *San Antonio Express-News*, was born "a rifle shot from the Alamo" and got his nickname during high school because he liked to sing "Red River Valley." In the early 1930s, as a teenager, he sang on some local radio stations, but then he hopped a freight train and made his way to Virginia where he was hired by a radio station as a singing cowboy.

At age twenty-one, he started writing "current events songs" or "topical songs," which would keep him busy for many years. His most famous song, one that would be performed countless times by fellow Texas eccentric Kinky Friedman, was "Amelia Earhart's Last Flight."

With a band called The Swift Cowboys, Red River Dave recorded a few albums, but his recording career was interrupted by a stint as a soldier during World War II. He hit musical gold during the war with patriotic songs like "I'd Like to Give My Dog to Uncle Sam" and "It's for God and Country and You Mom."

These musical successes were followed by a stretch in the late 1940s when Dave made a living as a B movie actor, appearing in Westerns such as *Swing in the Saddle* and *Echo Ranch*. In addition to singing and acting, other handy talents in Red River Dave's entertainment arsenal included rope tricks and yodeling (he had been a state champion yodeler in Texas as a youth).

A 1997 *Texas Monthly* article about "one of the longest careers in country music" states, "When commercial television debuted at the New York World's Fair in 1939, Red River Dave was there to broadcast live what is still his most famous creation [the Earhart song], along with other country and western songs, both traditional and original."

One Red River Dave website claims that this television appearance made the Texas singing cowboy the first ever paid television performer. The same website relates an event at a radio station in which Dave was handcuffed to a piano and, on a bet, came up with 52 original songs—lyrics and music—in an eight-hour period.

This story isn't hard to believe given that Red River Dave's greatest claim to fame was his ability to come up with spur of the moment songs about newsworthy events. His musical topics ranged from U2 pilot Gary Powers' spying trial to Patty

Hearst's abduction to the Apollo 11 incident. An obituary for Red River Dave in the UK's *The Independent* observed, "One of country music's great eccentrics, Red River Dave McEnery is best known for a seemingly inexhaustible string of 'event' songs written in response to the headlines of the day."

McEnery lived out his days in relative anonymity in Texas and often regaled friends and family with tales from his days at the dawn of modern popular culture. All but forgotten, he died in San Antonio in 2002.

Chapter 63

"Sister Shocked"

Michelle Shocked
1962-present

Name: Karen Michelle Johnston
Lived: 1962-present
Texas connection: Born in Dallas; raised in Gilmer
Occupation: Musician
Claim to weirdness: Her life
Tex-centricity Scale: 8 communes (out of 10)

According to the bio on her website, Michelle Shocked was raised in poverty in a strict fundamentalist Mormon household. Her father, who lived elsewhere, was a hippie and an atheist. She spent summers with him and enjoyed the freedom. When she reached college age, she put herself through the University of Texas at Austin on her own dime. After graduating, she hit the road and tramped around the country, eventually landing in

San Francisco. A photo of her resisting arrest during a 1984 protest of the Democratic National Convention landed on the front page of a San Fran paper. The photo would be used on her first American album cover.

A hardcore political activist in the 1980s and not yet a famous musician, Ms. Shocked sported a wild, spiked Mohawk and a nose ring. She was arrested a second time for obscenity at the 1984 Republican National Convention. After one of her activism-related arrests, police asked for her name, to which she replied "Michelle Shocked," a nod to the phrase "shell shocked," used to describe soldiers reeling from the realities of war.

In the aftermath of her arrests, Shocked was involuntarily committed by her mother to a mental hospital, where she received, ironically, electroshock therapy.

She spent the next several years wandering around the United States and Europe. In 1986, Shocked made her way back to Texas and, while playing some of her music around a campfire at the Kerrville Folk Festival, was recorded on a Sony Walkman by an Englishman who said he was a journalist.

The Englishman actually worked for an independent record label and soon released the unsuspecting American's music to the British public. The crude independent release—complete with crickets chirping in the background and trucks passing on a nearby highway—raced up the British charts. She performed her first concert in England not long after.

Back in the U.S., Shocked signed with a major label, Mercury, on the strength of the British release and released the ground-breaking *Short Sharp Shocked*. After a few more records, Shocked says her label told her they wouldn't honor her contract because she had cut too good a deal for herself. They refused to free her to work with another label and also refused to record her next project, a gospel album.

In a novel legal maneuver, Shocked sued the record company under the amendment that abolished slavery and, on the day the trial was to start, was released from her contract. As a result of her fearless confrontation with the mega-label, she is one of only a handful of major label artists who actually own their entire catalogue of music.

Shocked followed her three Mercury albums with releases on her own label. In 2007, she recorded a gospel album called *To Heaven U Ride*, and, at some point along the way, became a born-again Christian; this might be the strangest thing of all. Michelle Shocked, a former counter-culture punk rocker, leftist protester, feminist—after winning a New Music Award in 1989—had turned into a born-again Christian.

She became a regular attendee of an African-American Pentecostal church. Her fellow parishioners often call her "Our unique sister" and "Sister Shocked." The transformation was incredible. This same person had once recorded a song called "Campus Crusade," with lyrics that included "I'm gonna jump headfirst into that lake of fire...I think hell is gonna be just swell."

Stranger things have happened. Haven't they?

It appears that the conversion is legit. A not-particularly-interested-in-religion concertgoer in Portland wrote that Shocked "talked a lot about Jesus, but it was a positive message of love," and also noted that Shocked said she believes in a "radical liberation" of Christian theology from the right wing interpretation that many have of it.

What's next from Michelle Shocked? There is no telling. As she says in her online biography, "I can't tell you where I'm going...but I can tell you where I come from."

Chapter 64

"The Playmate"

Anna Nicole Smith
1967-2007

Name: Vicki Lynn Marshall (née Hogan)
Lived: 1962-2007
Texas connection: Born in Houston
Occupation: Model and actress
Claim to weirdness: Too dumb for 10th grade, but smart enough to marry a billionaire
Tex-centricity Scale: 7 prescription pills (out of 10)

Anna Nicole Smith started life as Vicki Lynn Hogan in Houston, Texas. After her parents split up, she went to live with her aunt in Mexia, Texas. She failed her freshman year in high school and dropped out to work at a fried chicken restaurant. In 1985, seventeen-year old Vicki married a sixteen-year-old cook at the restaurant. They had a son, Daniel, the following year and separated the year after that.

After taking her baby with her back to Houston, the woman who would become Anna Nicole Smith took a job as an exotic dancer. She soon answered a newspaper ad that called for ladies to audition for *Playboy* magazine. She rose to fame after she appeared on the cover of the March 1992 issue. She became a popular model for the racy magazine and took on the name Anna Nicole.

About five months before appearing on the cover of *Playboy* magazine, Smith had met octogenarian oil billionaire J. Howard Marshall at the Houston strip club where she worked. He romanced her for two years with expensive gifts and repeatedly asked her to marry him. She gave in and married him in 1994, giving rise to a chorus of gossip that she married him for his money. Not true, she maintained. It was for his looks. Just kidding. It was because she loved him.

Billions? What billions?

After Marshall's death, court cases raged in Texas, California, and Washington, D.C., regarding whether or not Anna Nicole Smith should receive a portion of Howard's legacy. She didn't appear in his will, but she asserted that Marshall had verbally promised her half of his estate. More than a decade after Marshall's death, even after Smith and E. Pearce Marshall (her chief opponent and her deceased husband's son) had both died, the lawsuit continued on behalf of their heirs.

During the years of her legal battle, Smith expanded her career from magazine and television model to include movies and her own reality television series. Critically lampooned for her acting skills, or lack thereof, she nonetheless acted in a half dozen movies, producing at least two of them.

Smith struggled with substance abuse and became notorious for erratic behavior. In 2004, she appeared on an awards show displaying the apparent effects of intoxication of some kind, slurring her speech and babbling nonsense.

Smith became pregnant in 2006 and gave birth to a daughter. Five men would eventually claim to be the father of Smith's daughter, including her lawyer, her former bodyguard and, oddly, Zsa Zsa Gabor's husband. After Dannielynn's birth in the Bahamas, Anna Nicole's son Daniel came to visit his mother and new sister in the hospital. He died mysteriously while in his mother's hospital room. An autopsy confirmed that Daniel died from a combination of drugs.

Bizarrely, Smith had a commitment ceremony with one of the men who claimed to be the father of Dannielynn only 18 days after her son's death.

Less than six months after her son's death, Anna Nicole herself died of an unintentional drug overdose. Subsequent investigations showed that she had 11 prescriptions, all of them prescribed in the names of various associates. But the Anna Nicole story was far from over.

News media carried endless stories about the fate of her infant daughter and the hundreds of millions of dollars that she might be due, depending upon the outcome of the ongoing lawsuits regarding J. Howard Marshall's estate. Then, two months after Anna Nicole Smith's death, a former boyfriend named Larry Birkhead was found to be the father of Dannielynn Smith, based on DNA testing.

Vicki Lynn Hogan, the high school dropout who had taken voice and modeling classes and had reinvented herself as a 21st century Marilyn Monroe, had, like her idol, lived an incredible life and met an early, tragic end. Like Monroe, Smith died with chloral hydrate in her system. And like Monroe, rumors and speculation continue to dog Smith even after her death.

Chapter 65

"Altered State of Mind"

(Sumner Erickson, Texcentrics lead singer.)
The Texcentrics
2005-present

Names: Sumner Erickson, Geno Gottschall, Mike Gottschall, and Buddy Forsythe
Active: 2005-present
Texas connection: Based in Austin
Occupation: Rock band
Claim to weirdness: Eclectic music and their moniker
Tex-centricity Scale: 5 Austin hippies (out of 10)

Okay, I'll confess that I don't know a whole lot about this band, except that the lead singer is Roky Erickson's brother. (Roky is profiled a few chapters back.) Despite my ignorance, I couldn't very well *not* include a band called the Texcentrics in a book about Texas eccentrics, could I?

Like his brother Roky, Sumner and his band play

"psychedelic country rock." That tidbit of weirdness alone qualifies them for inclusion here. Positive reviews for their live sets at Austin hotspots such as Threadgill's and The Hole in the Wall abound, with comparisons to fellow Texans Buddy Holly, Roy Orbison, and the like. The Texcentrics accept those comparisons, and also claim Texans like the Big Bopper, Stevie Ray Vaughan, and ZZ Top as influences. Performing songs with titles like "Altered State of Mind," they come by the psychedelic label honestly.

The Texcentrics stay busy playing the local bar scene, but also find themselves appearing at a variety of benefit concerts, including some organized to help raise money for Roky Erickson's trust fund and for organizations like CAEST (Coalition for the Abolition of Electroshock in Texas). They have also performed at Camp Casey, the anti-war campground near President Bush's ranch in Crawford, Texas, and they have appeared at Austin's renowned South by Southwest concert series.

The members of this little-known band with a great name have established themselves as princes of the oddball Austin music scene, and lead vocalist Sumner Erickson has earned the respect of the rock and roll community because, after he won custody of Roky, he greatly improved the care his brother received and helped him stand on his own two feet, with support.

The Texcentrics are eccentric, yes, but they're still good ol' boys, in the best sense of the phrase.

Chapter 66

"The Poet"

Townes Van Zandt
1944-1997

Name: Townes Van Zandt
Lived: 1944-1997
Texas connection: Born in Fort Worth
Occupation: Musician
Claim to weirdness: Self-destructive guitar poet
Tex-centricity Scale: 9 depressing songs (out of 10)

Townes Van Zandt, a distant descendant of Republic of Texas leader Isaac Van Zandt for whom Van Zandt county is named, was a child of oil wealth and privilege. While in college, on his way to a career in state politics, he got diverted toward a career in music instead.

Van Zandt was diagnosed with manic depression as a young adult and received insulin shock therapy, a therapy in which he was injected with massive doses of insulin and forced into a coma. The therapy is said to have erased most of his long term memory, and the sense of loneliness and isolation in many of his songs is attributed by many to this condition.

Van Zandt's greatest commercial success came in the form of royalty checks from his authorship of the hit song "Pancho and Lefty," a popular song performed most notably by Willie Nelson and Merle Haggard. He wrote songs for other artists as well. In fact, outlaw country singer Steve Earle called Van Zandt the "best songwriter in the world" and even offered to "stand on Bob Dylan's coffee table" to make that announcement. (Van Zandt retorted that he had met Dylan's bodyguards and was convinced that Steve Earle wouldn't get anywhere near Bob Dylan's coffee table.)

Van Zandt struggled with alcoholism all his life, as well as with drug addiction, depression and gambling. He also lived in itinerate poverty, despite the wealth of his family. He rambled all over the country, sometimes spending entire summers in the solitude of the Colorado woods, gallivanting around on horseback. For a time he lived in a Tennessee cabin with no indoor plumbing. He was also known to hop freight trains from time to time.

Van Zandt seemed to be most comfortable performing in front of tiny audiences, playing his incredibly sad folk-country-blues songs. By the end of his too-short 52-year life, Van Zandt was at once a living legend and an unknown—heralded among musicians as a song-writing savant while all but totally overlooked by mainstream country audiences.

He had thirty years in the music business behind him and had never recorded a single hit of his own. More often than not, other country and folk artists choose to call him a poet instead of a songwriter, emphasizing the clean, clear imagery and the heart-rending honesty often found in his lyrics.

After his death, interest in Townes Van Zandt spiked, as is typical with dead musicians. Several articles about the Texas

245

songwriter appeared in prominent industry magazines, along with a handful of books and the 2005 documentary *Be Here to Love Me*, the tagline of which, appropriately, is "What would you sacrifice to follow your dream?"

Chapter 67

"The Prodigy"

Stevie Ray Vaughan
1954-1990

Name: Stephen Ray Vaughan
Lived: 1954-1990
Texas connection: Born in Dallas
Occupation: *Rolling Stone* magazine's #7 Greatest Guitarist of All Time
Claim to weirdness: The Clint Eastwood clothes and superglued phalanges
Tex-centricity Scale: 4 ponchos (out of 10)

Stevie Ray Vaughan is widely remembered as a guitar virtuoso, a natural who never learned to read sheet music but could nonetheless make his guitar talk and his listeners weep. After falling in a tub of grease at the restaurant where he worked at age 17, he quit school and gave himself fully to his music. He had been playing the guitar for several years by then (he'd gotten his first lessons from his older brother Jimmie, who would famously play for the Fabulous Thunderbirds later on) and was already better than most adults.

Vaughan single-handedly ignited a blues revival in the mid-1980s—well, actually, he used both hands most of the time—and was one of the leaders in establishing Austin as the "Live Music Capital of the World."

Unlike many other blues artists in recent history, Vaughan actually experienced commercial success during his lifetime, selling out concerts regularly and producing a string of gold records. He toured all over the world and performed with many famous artists. He was nominated for many awards and won six Grammies from 1985 to 1993. He was honored with "Stevie Ray Vaughan Day" in Austin during his life; a statewide "Stevie Ray Vaughan Day" was announced by Texas Governor Ann Richards following his death. A statue of Vaughan stands in Austin to this day, and he has been inducted into the Blues Hall of Fame.

For several years early in his career, Vaughan struggled with alcohol abuse. He graduated to cocaine later but eventually kicked both habits with the help of a London doctor who had previously helped Eric Clapton and Pete Townsend overcome their addictions. Vaughan became a teetotaler and strictly avoided drugs and alcohol for the rest of his life.

Stevie Ray Vaughan wasn't as eccentric as some Texas musicians, though his guitar skills were clearly abnormal, in a good way. His otherworldly talent plus his sweat-dripping stage intensity and his wild getups made Vaughan a one-of-a-kind, instantly recognizable character on the national blues scene.

He often wore a poncho and almost always sported his "high roller" hat, as he called it, which was basically a cowboy hat with a flat brim and a flat crown, usually adorned with a band of shiny concho buckles around it.

Mark Beaty is a Texas school teacher who is a big enough fan of Stevie Ray Vaughan that he has kept a huge poster of the guitar hero in his classroom for years. When I asked Beaty if he thought of Vaughan as an eccentric, he said, "Well, he did Super Glue his fingers."

Huh?

Beaty explained that Vaughan would literally play until his fingers bled, and then, instead of stopping to heal, Stevie Ray would squirt Super Glue onto his fingertips to stop the flow and keep on jamming.

The bottle rocket ride to prominence that was Stevie Ray Vaughan's life would end all too soon. In August 1990, Vaughan and four other passengers boarded a helicopter after a concert in Wisconsin. Minutes after takeoff, the helicopter crashed into a ski slope, killing all aboard. Vaughan was a few months shy of 36 years old when he died.

The eclectic bluesman is gone, but he left his critically-acclaimed guitar licks for us to remember him by.

Chapter 68

"The Leading Buddy"

Owen Wilson
1968-present

Name: Owen Cunningham Wilson
Lived: 1968-present
Texas connection: Born in Dallas
Occupation: Actor
Claim to weirdness: Bizarre roles
Tex-centricity Scale: 7 broken noses (out of 10)

A college buddy of fellow Texas eccentric Wes Anderson, Owen Wilson graduated from the world of small, quirky independent movies like *Bottle Rocket* and *Rushmore* to become a Hollywood heavyweight. His strength has been as a comedic lead, and he has appeared in several $100-million-plus blockbuster films, including *Shanghai Noon*, *Wedding Crashers*, and the animated film *Cars*. He has also appeared frequently as a "leading buddy" in a number of "buddy films," movies in which Wilson as goofy, likeable sidekick serves up a steady stream of laughs.

Wilson's strength has been his ability to play easy-going, wisecracking characters—slackers, some have called his characters, or a "stoner's version of James Garner," to appropriate a phrase from the *New York Times*—guys who spout random silliness with a childlike earnestness that makes them all the more delightful. Whether playing a male model in *Zoolander* or an insecure train robber in *Shanghai Knights*, Wilson delivers a fun, light-hearted time, every time.

As his career heated up, Wilson quickly became a frequent subject of tabloid articles. One reason for this had to do with his romancing of a variety of young beauties. He was also profiled in entertainment publications along with his actor brother Luke due to their roles as founding members of the "Frat Pack," a group of prominent young actors that includes Jack Black, Vince Vaughn, Will Ferrell, Steve Carrell, and Ben Stiller, among others.

A 2003 article in *Texas Monthly* detailed Wilson's lightly checkered past: he got kicked out of an exclusive Dallas prep school for stealing the answers to a geometry test and not ratting out his collaborators. He also didn't exactly graduate from UT at Austin. (Doesn't seem to matter as much now, though, does it?) Nevertheless, the gist of the article was that Owen Wilson was solidly on Hollywood's A-list, an up-and-comer if ever there was one. And he was bringing his brothers Luke and Andrew along for the ride.

Entertainment press scrutiny of Owen Wilson only intensified in August 2007, after an apparent suicide attempt. The attempt would have garnered a great deal of media attention simply due to the fact that Wilson is a big star, but it was probably more newsworthy because Wilson had played a whole boatload of happy-go-lucky characters who seemed to bebop through their problems without a care in the world.

It was hard for movie fans to think of Owen Wilson being suicidal, since what they had seen of him had always been so carefree.

Since then, Wilson has bounced back from his dark times admirably. He made a public appearance at the premiere of *The Darjeeling Limited*, an oddball film he made with oddball friend Anderson. Then he continued his work on a number of projects.

Wilson's status among Texas eccentrics is assured, though not as a result of his dark days. Wilson is a lock because of his contributions as both a screenwriter and an actor to the bizarre cinematic creations of Wes Anderson, art house flicks that somehow manage to find a rabid audience and, not surprisingly, impress out-of-touch-with-regular-people critics.

What sets Wilson apart from other artsy-fartsy actors is his ability to successfully break out of the mold of starving independent film actor and become a true Hollywood superstar, while staying true to his roots on the art house movie scene. It remains to be seen if his star will shine as brightly in the future, but the smart money says it will.

Chapter 69

"Avant-Garde Visionary"

Robert Wilson
1941-present

Name: Robert Wilson
Lived: 1941-present
Texas connection: Born in Waco
Occupation: Experimental theater director
Claim to weirdness: There's nothing weird about avant-garde theater, is there?
Tex-centricity Scale: 8 wordless plays (out of 10)

While I have never looked up the term "avant-garde" in a French-English dictionary, I would be willing to venture that it probably means "weird." I readily admit that I am one of those clods who don't know how to appreciate Jackson Pollock's paint splatters or William Carlos Williams' 16-word masterpiece of poetry about a red wheelbarrow. I freely grant that I'm clueless as to why Andy Warhol's painting of a soup can is any more inspiring than an actual soup can. So maybe I'm not the best one to write about the international king of avant-garde theater.

But I'm going to anyway.

Robert Wilson was born in the hotbed of progressive thought that is Waco, Texas (see Kermit Oliver a few chapters back if you don't believe me), and he studied Business Administration at UT before moving to New York to pursue an architecture degree.

In 1968, Wilson founded an experimental theater troupe, as most architects do. After creating a series of envelope-shredding plays and operas, he worked with Philip Glass to create *Einstein on the Beach*, a 1970s opera that achieved worldwide acclaim for both men. (It is one of the most famous operas that I've never heard of.)

Wilson followed this success with ever more daring and, some might say, bizarre productions. In the 1980s he created a six-part, 12-hour opera about the American Civil War for the 1984 Summer Olympics. The project was cancelled due to cost overruns, missed deadlines, and other unspecified issues. Though it has never been performed in its entirety, all six parts have since been publicly performed at different times and in different places.

Wilson's other productions have included a 12-hour show about Josef Stalin and, perhaps strangest of all, a seven-day production on a mountaintop in Iran. He started one play with a fifteen-minute silent prologue while another of his creations, *Deafman Glance*, contained no words at all. In yet another work, Wilson had two characters speak the exact same lines with different tones, attitudes, and movements, resulting in two completely different realities, in order to show that words alone do not create meaning. I have to admit that that's a pretty cool idea.

Wilson's artistic vision is not restricted to writing scripts and directing plays and operas, however. He is a dancer and an award-winning sculptor. His drawings and furniture designs have appeared in museums and galleries around the world. In the early 2000s, he produced a series of highly-regarded videos starring the likes of Brad Pitt and Winona Rider for an experimental high definition cable channel.

Robert Wilson is an avant-garde Renaissance man.

Few people in the world—and by few, I mean none—are as acclaimed as Robert Wilson in the world of avant-garde theater.

Eugene Ionesco, an absurdist playwright, has said Wilson was greater than Nobel Prize-winning playwright Samuel Beckett. (He was apparently not being absurd when he said this.) The *New York Times* labeled Wilson "a towering figure." As far as I know, he is actually of a very average height, physically speaking.

Wilson has been honored with dozens of awards in Europe and at home, and he continues to produce theater that the erudite of the world find exceptional and the morons of the world (present company included) find inexplicable.

I still think that avant-garde means weird, but even weirder than that is that the king of the avant-garde was born in Waco. It just goes to prove that Texas—despite what out-of-state snobs might want to believe—is the real capital of unique thought and eccentricity.

Just as we Texans have suspected all along.

Chapter 70

"That Little Ol' Band from Texas"

ZZ Top
1969-present

Names: Billy Gibbons, Dusty Hill, and Frank Beard
Active: 1969-present
Texas connection: Formed in Houston
Occupation: Blues rockers
Claim to weirdness: Longest beards in rock and roll
Tex-centricity Scale: 4 classic hot rods (out of 10)

When the Gillette company offered Billy Gibbons and Dusty Hill $1 million dollars apiece to shave their famous beards on a commercial, they both declined. Their reasoning: "We're too ugly without 'em."

ZZ Top got its start after two members of the popular Houston band Moving Sidewalks were drafted into the U.S. Army. Billy Gibbons found new band mates by luring Dusty

Hill and Frank Beard away from American Blues, another Houston band. Gibbons and company had scored two Top Ten hits with Moving Sidewalks; many more hit songs would come with ZZ Top.

There are two things that set ZZ Top apart from all other bands. The first is their characteristic sound—a unique guitar-driven rocking blues. A ZZ Top song is instantly recognizable. (And so is a ZZ Top video, for that matter, in that most involve classic hot rods and beautiful women in revealing clothes.)

The second thing that makes ZZ Top unique—eccentric, you might even say—is their trademark look, particularly the fact that two members (Billy Gibbons and Dusty Hill) sport chest-length beards. (No word on the level of popularity ZZ Top enjoys among Sikhs and the Amish.)

Ironically, the only member of ZZ Top without a beard is, you guessed it, Frank Beard. According to ZZ Top lore, the other two band members grew their beards independently of one another during a two-and-a-half year break from touring and recording and have kept them ever since. Gibbons' and Hill's unique look is topped off by dark sunglasses and hats, because every girl's crazy about a sharp-dressed man.

But it isn't the look that has made people buy ZZ Top albums: it's the sound. And buy them they have: *Eliminator* was 10-times platinum, and *Afterburner* was five-times platinum. Three other ZZ Top albums have gone platinum, and four gold. The members of ZZ Top excel as musicians, obviously. Lead singer and guitarist Billy Gibbons was once said to be the favorite guitarist of none other than Jimi Hendrix.

Billy Gibbons once said that the name ZZ Top was a convoluted tribute to blues legend B.B. King—they wanted to call themselves ZZ King, but decided it sounded too similar to the target of their praise. They changed King to Top, and there you have it. (Some folks don't buy this story. Other theories are that the name is short for Zig Zag and Top, two brands of rolling papers; that it's a tribute to bluesman Z.Z. Hill; or that it stems from some words on a billboard that ran together when one of the band members looked at them.)

In a particularly unconventional move, the members of ZZ Top were among the first donors to step up and help save Houston's iconic Orange Show—a conglomeration of brightly-painted metal structures and second-hand junk designed as a poor man's theme park and built in honor of that most popular of citrus fruits, the orange. ZZ Top donated money to preserve the screwball eyesore from demolition.

Famous for songs like "Sharp Dressed Man," "Legs," and "Gimme All Your Lovin'," ZZ Top is an original, a symbol of Texas cool, and one of very few bands in the history of rock and roll to perform with the same lineup for over 30 years.

Weird, yes; but definitely cool.

Part 5
Other Oddballs

There are many eccentrics in Texas who do not necessarily fall into a neat category. In this section, you will read about a variety of Texans whose weirdness is hard to put a label on.

Amarillo Slim

(b. 1928; lives in Amarillo, of course) Amarillo Slim (real name: Thomas Preston, Jr.) is a professional poker player, winner of the 1972 World Series of Poker, and an inductee into the Poker Hall of Fame. Helping to open a casino in South America, Slim was once kidnapped by Colombian drug lord Pablo Escobar. He was released shortly thereafter, as he wasn't the gringo they were looking for. Nicolas Cage is set to play him in a movie about his life.

Jedge Arbuckle

(1866-1931; born in San Antonio; real name: Maclyn Arbuckle) Arbuckle was a well-known stage actor in the late 1800s. He was a cousin to silent film star Roscoe "Fatty" Arbuckle. In 1918, Jedge Arbuckle started a motion picture company of his own in San Antonio and starred in several films. Arbuckle didn't start out so successfully, however. After not making it into Harvard and rebelling against his father's notion that he be a clergyman, Arbuckle bounced from pharmacy work to office work to farm work to legal work. Arbuckle's true love during this time was Shakespeare, and once, while running for Justice of the Peace, he took to reciting long passages from the Bard's plays in the bars of Bowie County. It was then that he earned the nickname "Jedge." His acting career started in Louisiana shortly after his failed run for public office—turns out that bar patrons don't always show up to vote in great numbers—but it eventually took him to San

259

Francisco, New York, and even to Europe. No word on whether Jon Arbuckle of *Garfield* fame is related.

Madge Bellamy
(1899-1990; born in Hillsboro, Texas) After running away to New York City at age 17, Madge Bellamy managed to become a leading actress of the 1920s. Her most famous role came in 1932 when she starred opposite Bela Lugosi in the film *White Zombie*. Bellamy had a reputation as a diva and as a wild partier. Her acting career came to a screeching halt in 1943 after she shot a lover. In the aftermath, Bellamy was reported to have said, "I only winged him." She died in California in 1990; her memoirs, entitled *A Darling of the Twenties,* came out shortly after her death.

Boxcar Willie
(1931-1999; born in Sterrett, Texas) Lecil Martin, Air Force flier, became Boxcar Willie, hobo singer, at a talent show in San Jose, California in which he won first prize. He went on to sell more than 10 million albums and was one of the first major entertainers to open a theater in Branson, Missouri, where he also owned motels and a train museum.

Joe Bob Briggs
(b. 1953 in Dallas; real name: John Irving Bloom) Briggs rose to national prominence by writing humorous redneck-flavored B-movie reviews for *Texas Monthly* and later, in syndication. A one-man show evolved, *Joe Bob's Drive-In Theater*, a program that became the highest-rated show on The Movie Channel for several years. More recently, Briggs has been a part of the religious satire webzine *The Wittenburg Door* ("Whittenburg" is deliberately misspelled in the title.) Briggs has written several books and contributed to a number of DVDs related to cult movie classics.

Burrell Cannon

(1848-1922; lived in Pittsburg, Texas) Cannon, a Baptist pastor, was inspired by the Biblical book of Ezekiel to build what he dubbed "The Ezekiel Airship." Built with the proceeds of a $20,000 stock sale, the airship was constructed based on the words, "Their appearance was as it were a wheel within the middle of the wheel" (Ezekiel 1:16). Cannon's ship—a full-size model of which is now on display in Pittsburg—was powered by paddles on concentric wheels. Pittsburg residents as late as the 1960s claimed to have seen the strange craft fly prior to the Wright brothers' famous flight at Kitty Hawk, North Carolina. The contraption was destroyed when a strong wind blew it off a rail car during transport to St. Louis where it was to be displayed.

Bobcat Carter

Carter lived in Texas' Big Bend and was known for roadside back flips and cartwheels. The eccentric old timer was also known for his questionable hygiene—that fact alone makes him my favorite character in this book. He proclaimed that he took a bath once every seven years, whether he needed it or not. To accentuate the smell, he ate skunk stew. According to legend, he died at 100 from pneumonia after doctors at an Alpine hospital insisted on giving him a bath.

Leslie Cochran

(b. 1951; lives in Austin; real name: Al Leslie Cochran) Cochran is a cross-dressing homeless man who epitomizes the "Keep Austin Weird" movement. He has run for mayor several times, once finishing second, and has participated in many events benefitting social causes. He has been an unofficial spokesman for the homeless in Austin for several years and can be seen regularly on Sixth Street, more often than not in women's clothing.

Douglas "Wrong Way" Corrigan

(1907-1995; born in Galveston) Corrigan became a national hero after "accidentally" flying solo to Ireland from New York in 1938. After a flight from California to New York, Corrigan was supposed to fly back to the West Coast but claimed that he got confused due to cloud cover and headed the wrong way. He didn't realize his error until 26 hours into the flight when it became apparent that there wasn't, you know, any land below him.

Corrigan made the flight in an airplane that was hardly in tip-top shape—fuel began leaking into the cabin at one point and Corrigan had to punch a hole in the floor with a screwdriver to let it drain so that the fumes wouldn't asphyxiate him. (Asphyxiation is generally a very bad thing, except in Scrabble.) Before his record- and statute-breaking flight, Corrigan had applied to the FAA multiple times for permission to fly across the Atlantic, to no avail.

After the "accidental" flight, he was sent back to the U.S. from Ireland via ocean liner, where he was welcomed to New York with a ticker tape parade. Later he published an autobiography entitled *That's My Story.* Some reports say that he earned $75,000 from his newfound fame.

Jimmy Dean

(b. 1928 in Plainview, Texas) Jimmy Dean was a famous singer and actor from the 1940s through the 1960s. In 1969, he did what many aging stars do—he transitioned from entertainer to sausage mogul. He did this by forming the Jimmy Dean Sausage Company. The sausage business proved lucrative for Dean, and he appeared in television commercials for his company for years. As far as this author knows, Jimmy Dean has sold more sausage than any other Grammy award-winning recording artist, ever.

Larry Dennis

Dennis, the owner of Texas Hill Country Furniture and Mercantile on Highway 281 between Stephenville and Mineral Wells, is also the proud owner of the Star of Texas Rocking Chair, which he claims is the largest rocker in the world. (I thought that honor belonged to Meat Loaf, who is featured a few pages back, but I stand corrected.) The Star of Texas stands almost three stories high and weighs four tons. Meat Loaf weighs considerably less.

Carlos Esparza

(1828-1885) Esparza, along with his rancher father and other citizens, attempted to establish an autonomous region called the Territory of the Rio Grande in South Texas. The separatist movement was intended to protect the interests of Mexican-Americans who supported Juan Cortina. Esparza assisted both Confederate and Union forces during the Civil War, all the while providing materials and support to the Cortinistas. After Juan Cortina was arrested in 1875, Esparza kept a low profile and lived out his days on his ranch.

Billy Sol Estes

(b. 1924 in Abilene) Estes came to prominence as a West Texas conman without equal, several of whose associates died under mysterious circumstances. Estes is also known for accusing another of his acquaintances, President Lyndon Johnson, of being a party to the assassination of JFK. Estes' descent into fraud began when he started claiming massive supplies of cotton and anhydrous ammonia as collateral for bank loans. The problem was, these supplies never existed. Estes was sent to prison. In the 1980s, Estes' lawyer sent a letter to government officials claiming that Estes and LBJ had been involved in the murders of no fewer than nine people, including President Kennedy and Lyndon Johnson's sister Josefa.

Moses Evans

(1812-1853; lived in Washington-on-the-Brazos) Evans sported a long red beard and wore a rattlesnake skin vest. In South Texas in the mid 1800s he was known as "The Wild Man of the Woods." He grew somewhat famous after the reported appearance of a "Wild Woman" in the same area. Overzealous journalists created rapturous love letters between the two wild people and published them in local newspapers. The amorous communiqués were soon reproduced in newspapers back East, and Evans' reputation as a woodsy Don Juan was secured. According to the *Handbook of Texas Online*, Evans actually caught the "Wild Woman of the Navidad" at one point and discovered that "she" was actually a "he"—a runaway male slave. Later in his life, Evans became a hellfire-and-brimstone Methodist preacher, and made quite an impression on lost souls with his outrageous appearance.

Gilbert Felts

(d. 1989; lived in Terlingua, Texas) Sometime in the early 1980s, Gilbert Felts decided to open a bar and restaurant in a cave in the desert town of Terlingua. He named the place "La Kiva," after a subterranean ceremonial room used by Pueblo Indians. *GQ* magazine has called La Kiva "the #1 most bizarre bar you must visit before you die." La Kiva has been featured in two documentaries and favorably reviewed in a number of respected publications, including once being named one of the 50 best bars in America. The unofficial mascot of La Kiva is a faux fossilized cat skeleton affectionately known by a completely inappropriate name that I won't record here. As of this writing, the strange bar is for sale.

Fred Felty

Molino del Santo (Santo's Mill) in Gibraltar was once nothing more than an abandoned old flour and olive oil mill. Now it is an exclusive hotel—it costs up to 180 Euros per night for a suite. Apparently, a Euro is some kind of foreign money. For a time, the old mill was home to an eccentric Texan named Fred Felty. Felty, an expatriate lawyer, worked at a nearby American naval base. He came across the abandoned mill in 1970 on a day off and bought it for a weekend getaway. Over the years, he spent his time repairing it. He lived intermittently in the old mill and filled it up with all manner of odds and ends. He sold it to four British school teachers in 1986 and moved back to the U.S. of A. And that's all I know about Fred Felty.

John W. Gates

(1855-1911) Gates, who was worth an estimated $40 million at the time of his death, got his start in business in San Antonio, Texas, selling barbed wire. A natural promoter, he started his own successful wire company in St. Louis, Missouri, and joined with another company in 1898 to form a wire monopoly. He later helped start Texaco and tried his hand in the railroad business. Gates, an avid gambler, obtained the nickname "Bet-A-Million" after winning several hundred thousand dollars betting on a single horse race and by participating in a legendary poker game during a train ride from Chicago to New York.

Vince Hanneman

Austin resident Hanneman created a "Cathedral of Junk" behind his house, for unknown reasons. Invisible from the street, the tower of trash virtually fills his entire backyard. The multi-level structure includes a throne room and staircases to observation platforms. Any attempt to catalogue the kinds of junk used in the cathedral's construction would fall woefully short. Suffice it to say, most of it is metal, and some of the electrical castoffs embedded in the walls still work. Neighbors have complained to city officials, who in turn have sent engineers to study the giant pile of refuse. Hanneman has considered tearing down his work of art, but so far it is still standing.

Blind Lemon Jefferson
(1894-1929; born in Coutchman, Texas) Blind from birth, Lemon Henry Jefferson became an acclaimed blues singer in the 1920s. Jefferson released 43 records from 1926 to 1929. Many of his songs were major national hits. Some sold hundreds of thousands of copies. Jefferson was given a car by Paramount Records and possibly earned enough to hire a chauffer. He died in Chicago in 1929 under mysterious circumstances. Some say he froze to death; others contend he was poisoned by a jilted lover; still others hold that he had a heart attack or that he was murdered by a guide taking him (and his large royalty payment) to a train station to catch a ride back to Texas.

Vendyl Jones
(b. 1930 in Sudan, Texas) Jones, a former Baptist pastor, became interested in the Jewish history of the Bible and soon left the traditional Christian ministry to pursue studies under a series of rabbis. He became a Noahide—a non-Jew who follows the Seven Laws of Noah—and eventually relocated to Israel. Once there, Jones began leading archaeological expeditions, with a particular focus on searching for Biblical artifacts, including the Ark of the Covenant. Some of Jones' claims regarding purported discoveries have been disputed by other archaeologists. For a time, Jones claimed that the movie character Indiana Jones was based on his life. This was also disputed, and Vendyl Jones apparently no longer makes this claim.

Leadbelly
(1888-1949; moved to East Texas when he was 10) Huddie Ledbetter, better known as Leadbelly, was a 12-string guitar

virtuoso and a convicted murderer. His first prison sentence came in 1918, when he was sentenced to 30 years in the Texas penitentiary. He was pardoned in 1925 after having written a song in honor of Texas governor Pat Neff.

He tried out the Louisiana prison system in 1930, going to Angola, Louisiana on a charge of assault with intent to murder. Texas folklorist and musicologist John Lomax got him freed this time, and he toured the country playing the blues until 1939, when he went to Riker's Island for assault.

When he wasn't locked up, Leadbelly was a prolific minstrel, writing over 300 songs, dozens of which have been covered by prominent artists over the years. Leadbelly's distinctive nickname is the subject of much speculation. Some have said it derived from his ability to drink impressive quantities of prison hooch, or from having been shot in the stomach, or from his ability to take a punch.

Charles and Sandra McKee

(live in Waxahachie, Texas) The McKees built a house in Waxahachie that is a nearly-exact replica of the television home of the Munster family. It's accurate both inside and out, with a revolving suit of armor that leads to a secret room, a staircase that opens, and a basement laboratory. Construction of the odd house cost a mere quarter of a million dollars.

Jeff McKissack

(1902-1980; lived in Houston) McKissack was a mailman in Houston who believed in good nutrition. He spent 20 years building a "health show," as he called The Orange Show. Made up of mazes, metal art, railings, platforms, and a variety of reclaimed junk, all of it painted in bright carnival colors, the show was highlighted by displays that touted the qualities of everyone's favorite orange fruit, the orange. Sadly, after spending 20 years building the site, McKissack died only one year after opening it to the public. The Orange Show is now

267

maintained by a local foundation and is used for a variety of artistic purposes.

John Milkovisch

A retired railroad worker, Milkovisch staved off the boredom that some associate with retirement by drinking lots of beer and then using all the dead soldiers to decorate his home. He used smashed beer cans as siding, linked pull tabs as curtains, and long rows of cans as partitions. Though Milkovisch has since passed away, his Beer Can House still stands in a residential neighborhood in Houston.

O. L. Nelms

(1908-1972) When Nelms married his wife, Lillian, he only had five dollars to his name. Together, the couple became tobacco and candy wholesalers, starting from the ground up. Over time they became millionaires and real estate moguls. They donated large sums to local charities and churches and, as if this weren't enough to demonstrate their appreciation, O. L. Nelms had semi-trailers parked all over Dallas, the sides of which read, "Thanks all of you for helping O. L. Nelms make another million." A 1969 *Time* magazine article told of Nelms' plan to establish a fund for an endless series of beer bashes after his death—"with free food and drink for anyone who wants to attend." Nelms bought an office building to have the parties in and a lot for parking. He also arranged with a Dallas funeral home to have his remains brought out in a silver casket at each party, and instructed that his remains stay at the party until the last guests departed.

Though it appears that these parties never materialized, some of Nelms' last requests were indeed honored, including that he be buried with a six pack of Budweiser by his side, some King Edward cigars in his front pocket, and a bolo tie around his neck. (Apparently, some people *would* be caught dead in a bolo tie.)

O. T. Nodrog

O. T. Nodrog was the adopted name of one Orville T. Gordon, the leader of a Weslaco, Texas-based doomsday cult. The enigmatic Nodrog, last seen in his nineties and since assumed deceased, headed up a group known alternatively as the Outer-Dimensional Forces (O. D. F.) or as the Armageddon Time Ark Base Operation. The group seemed to believe that they were attacked by the CIA in the 1970s, that the Outer Dimensional Forces (aliens) returned to Earth in 1966 (and were angered at humans' mismanagement of the planet), and that Earth would be purged by these aliens after members of the cult were rescued. The rescue via flying saucers was expected in 1999. The group hasn't been heard from in recent years, which clearly indicates that they were indeed rescued by aliens in 1999 and the rest of us are screwed.

William Sydney Porter

(1862-1910) Better known by his pen name O. Henry, Porter was a bank teller in Cisco, Texas; he also lived in Austin. After being accused of embezzlement, Porter fled to Honduras. He returned to Texas when he learned that his wife was dying and that freedom in Honduras was worse than prison in America. Porter got five years behind bars, where he perfected his style of writing.

Within three years of his release, O. Henry had become a world-famous short story author. (The stories were short—I don't know how tall O. Henry was.) He moved to New York and published over 300 works. Despite his prolific output, he died a penniless alcoholic at 47 years of age.

Brushy Bill Roberts

(1879?-1950; died in Hico, Texas) Roberts claimed a few years before his death that his true identity was William H. Bonney, better known as Billy the Kid. While these claims are disputed by most historians, some studies have proved inconclusive. In one case, a lawyer named Morrison allegedly met with Roberts and saw dozens of scars from gunshot and knife wounds which matched descriptions of wounds known to exist on Billy the Kid. Morrison reportedly took Roberts to visit a number of Billy the Kid's acquaintances, many of whom signed affidavits attesting to the veracity of the Brushy Bill Roberts story. Morrison even arranged a meeting with a New Mexico governor to request a pardon that had been promised to Billy the Kid before his supposed death. The governor didn't buy the story, and the pardon wasn't granted. Roberts died of a heart attack not long after.

Al Shepperd
(d. 1994) Shepperd was given a leftover slab of limestone by a neighbor in 1989 and was subsequently inspired to build Stonehenge II. His version of the mysterious British tourist trap is only slightly smaller, but a whole lot closer. After finishing Stonehenge II, Shepperd added two giant heads (think Easter Island). His creations can be found northwest of San Antonio.

Barney Smith
In Alamo Heights, Texas, one can find Barney Smith's Toilet Seat Art Museum. Including over 700 painted or otherwise decorated toilet seats, the museum showcases Smith's passion. A retired plumber, Smith started his collection by mounting deer antlers onto an old toilet seat. Hundreds of seats followed, as did interviews on the local news, *Montel*, and even *The Today Show.*

Walter "Buck" Swords
(c. 1918-2007; lived in Brownsville, Texas) Swords was a cantankerous and foul-mouthed frequent customer at the Luby's Restaurant where waitress Melina Salazar made her living. Salazar put up with his misbehavior for seven years before he died. And then, when the 89-year-old passed away in

2007, he left her $50,000 and a 2000-model Buick. Salazar presumably went from being glad the mean old man had died to being *really* glad the mean old man had died.

Simon Vega

Simon Vega loved Elvis Presley so much that he turned his own house into Little Graceland in Los Fresnos, Texas. Vega had been a fan of the King's music, but his appreciation increased when Vega served with Elvis at Fort Hood. Vega admits that he didn't talk to Elvis much during basic training, but when the two men were shipped to Germany, they roomed together in the barracks. After Elvis' death, Vega responded by buying every piece of memorabilia he could find as a tribute to his friend. Eventually, he put gates just like the ones at the real Graceland in front of his house. Since then, people haven't stopped visiting.

Lizzie Williams

(1840-1924) Williams got her start as a school teacher but eventually, after keeping books for cattlemen, realized there was more profit to be made in raising cattle than in teaching school. Besides, cows don't sass back.

She bought land, registered a brand, and became the first woman to ride the Chisholm Trail with cattle carrying her own brand. She eventually became known as Texas' "Cattle Queen" and signed an early form of a pre-nuptial agreement when she married, allowing her to retain control of her property and finances. After the death of her husband, Williams became a recluse and a miser. When she died, locals were surprised that she was worth close to $250,000.

Wolfman Jack

(1938-1995; real name: Robert Weston Smith) A native New Yorker, Wolfman Jack got his start in radio in Del Rio, Texas, where a memorial was erected after his death. Wolfman

Jack, a rock and roll radio disc jockey, was internationally known in the 1960s and 1970s. His gravelly voice and bushy Wolfman persona made him a celebrity.

He had a key role in the George Lucas film *American Graffiti* and later appeared in a variety of television shows and commercials, and his voice appeared in a number of songs and provided the narration to at least one arcade game. An iconic figure of American radio, Wolfman Jack died of a heart attack in California at age 57